Crystal Ball Reading

For Beginners

About Alexandra Chauran

Alexandra Chauran is a second-generation professional fortuneteller. She has been reading the crystal ball professionally since 1999. Holding a Master's degree in teaching from Seattle University, she enjoys building carefully upon what is already understood by the student, and she offers an apprentice internship to her local practice in the greater Seattle area. Alexandra is also proficient in other forms of divination, having been certified as a Professional Tarot Reader by the Tarot Certification Board of the American Tarot Association. She writes horoscopes and other articles for periodic publications, and has appeared on National Public Radio's *Morning Edition*.

Please visit her website, at http://www.earthshod.com.

Crystal Ball Reading

For Beginners

Easy Divination & Interpretation

ALEXANDRA CHAURAN

Llewellyn Publications
Woodbury, Minnesota

First Edition
First Printing, 2011

Cover design by Adrienne Zimiga
Cover image © PhotoAlto Agency RF Collections/PunchStock

Llewellyn is a registered trademark of Llewellyn Worldwide Ltd.

Chauran, Alexandra, 1981–
    Crystal ball reading for beginners : easy divination & interpretation / Alexandra Chauran. — 1st ed.
        p.   cm.
    Includes bibliographical references and index.
    ISBN 978-0-7387-2626-7
    1. Crystal gazing. I. Title.
    BF1335.C43 2011
    133.3'22—dc22
                                                        2011004836

Llewellyn Publications
A Division of Llewellyn Worldwide Ltd.
2143 Wooddale Drive
Woodbury, MN 55125-2989
www.llewellyn.com

Printed in the United States of America

contents

The names and identifying details of the people in the vignettes and anecdotes in this book have been changed in order to protect the anonymity of clients.

introduction

"Hello, my name is Alexandra, and I'm the fortune-teller," I said as I arrived, toting my crystal ball, at the home of a woman celebrating her engagement, where she had gathered a dozen friends for an intimate celebration.

As I was ushered into her home, the comfortable clamor of friends excitedly talking became noticeably subdued as timid eyes sized me up. I was twenty-six years old, slender, and clad in a white dress. I entered the house barefoot, even though the weather had been brisk outside. Aside from my preferred barefoot state, there was nothing unusual about my appearance. My outfit was professional; my dark, shoulder-length hair was left in its naturally curly state, and my makeup and jewelry was minimal. I looked like just another guest.

I might easily have melted into the group's merry conversation over snacks if the guest of honor hadn't instructed me to let them know why I was there. I introduced myself to the group and gave a brief introduction to a type of fortunetelling called *crystalomancy*, explaining that, for people with problems with love or career, or any other area of life, divination offered practical solutions through the use of our intuition. I let them know that this evening I would be using a real crystal ball to confirm some things they already knew, to discover new potential in their lives, and to empower them with advice.

After such a bold speech, the guests were even more nervous. But the hostess allowed me to stick around and mingle while a few glasses of wine gave them courage. At last, the bravest of the bunch walked with me to a private area that the hostess had designated for readings, followed later by the rest of the excited guests once they had a chance to hear what she had to say about my reading. Over the course of the evening, I predicted children, extreme job changes, moves to distant lands, and even a few breakups to those who knew they needed to hear such news. By the end of the night, my table was crowded with everyone needing "just one more" reading.

How I Got Started

Teaching crystal ball reading is an unusual trade, even more so than telling fortunes using a crystal ball. In fact, I know of no others besides myself who currently offer local apprenticeships for learning how to perform this art. Though I learned how to read crystal balls at an early age with natural inclination, guidance from spiritual teachers, encouragement from parents, and a little bit of luck, it was only many years later that I began to pass on the knowledge that I've gained.

At first, with a bit of an ego, I assumed that I had special powers. But, given time and experience with others reading the crystal ball for me, I began to believe that everyone has the potential to practice this art. Some stumble upon their talents early; others must work hard on the discipline to achieve them; and still others actively work against developing such skills. My path in life has continuously drawn me into a teaching role, even when I struggled against it. With regard to the crystal ball, it began as a teenager when friends begged me to show them how I did it. An inability to understand how they might be different from me in their use of the crystal ball, as well as possibly a bit of self-sabotage in order to keep feeling special with my unique activity, kept us all frustrated for a while.

In college, I began to learn about psychology and the language of symbols that permeates all societies. Fascinated with how this was a common part of the human condition, and how it could be directly related to crystal ball reading, I hungrily studied symbols in many cultures and the common storylines that arose again and again. Just as I recognized the Hero's Journey in many stories, retelling the epic journey of someone going to another realm to bring back treasure, I realized that it was going to be my own task to bring back my own experiences from the crystal ball so that others could share in these universal understandings.

I learned that Carl Jung, the founder of analytical psychology, believed that the mind holds keys for how we work through problems in everyday life. The prominent psychologist used dream interpretation as a way to help people move through this world of symbols to understand how best to solve their own issues. Crystal ball gazing is very much like interpreting dreams that you are having while you are wide awake, and so it has the benefit of a deeper understanding of psychology.

Later thinkers, like mythologist Joseph Campbell, believed that symbols and archetypes found in repeating patterns in stories throughout history reflect the archetypes in the lives of real people. His catchphrase was "Follow your bliss." When you march along with the flow of your destiny, which is this theoretical structure that follows the archetypes in the Hero's Journey played out in mythology, it can seem like every challenge is lighter upon your shoulders. Understanding archetypes in the crystal ball can help you flow along your path more easily by pointing the way that is best for you.

For example, I often drive a long distance to visit my spiritual peers and elders. Others might find the traffic, gas money, and time to be frustrating enough to avoid training in this way. But for me, it's not really an issue. I'm following my bliss, and any challenge in the way seems relatively easy to overcome when I put my mind to it. However, if I was traveling all that way for, say, a dental appointment, I might whine about the traffic all the time, and even find it a reason to quit. Dental work isn't my bliss! Everyone's true desire is different, which is why you might see so many of your friends enduring relationship squabbles that would be a dealbreaker for you, while refusing to tolerate annoying aspects of partners that you find endearing and easy to overlook! Let's just say that following one's bliss is as easy as falling in love.

So, what if you don't know what your "bliss" is, or how to follow it? That's where the symbology of your dreams and the crystal ball can help when they are interpreted as a psychological aid. Although divination tools can and are used by many therapists, I often joke to my friends that, as a fortuneteller, "I'm like a therapist, only I actually help people." There are very real emotional and intellectual benefits to getting to know yourself through a crystal ball.

You see, your subconscious knows, but your subconscious isn't talking to you from the place of language and your left-brained cognition. Instead, your subconscious talks to you through symbols that you can see in the crystal ball. For example, when choosing between two lovers, a man might envision in the crystal ball a heart next to the woman he should choose, who would be best for him, even if his conscious mind hasn't been made up. He might also see some symbols that help him think about things he had not yet considered, such as how the second woman's goals might diverge sharply from his own, symbolized as her face surrounded by cars and material objects that he would not be able to afford to buy for her.

The crystal ball can also be used to examine someone's personality, and to correct emotional disorders in the exact same way as the Rorschach inkblot test is used. The Rorschach test is widely used by clinical psychologists to analyze personality, thought process, motivations, and conflicts, and I believe that the crystal ball would be an even more powerful tool for use by psychotherapists and their patients. It is like an infinite database of such inkblots, freeing the practitioner from the cultural bias and other sources of error that limit the Rorschach scoring systems.

The crystal ball can be used by both the spiritual and the nonspiritual as a psychological tool to access your subconscious through your right brain, to identify your problems and the solutions to those problems so that you can make choices to run your life. Even for the deeply religious, this process is still going on, adding an extra dimension to the usefulness of crystal ball reading.

I felt during my first experience of crystal ball reading, and still feel, that the crystal ball is a uniquely marvelous tool for divination, because it is like a direct window to one's own subconscious mind. The beginner doesn't have to force somebody else's system to make sense. Instead, the beginner can immediately start to piece together his or her own system and learn an internal language of symbols that have been building since birth, and maybe even before that. At the outset, that may seem the more difficult route, and in some ways it is more challenging since it involves constant growth and reevaluation. But, on the other hand, it requires less rote memorization, and better equips the beginner to transfer those skills to other forms of divination, or even to apply those skills to existing life experiences such as dreams or visions that might otherwise be troubling and confusing.

After graduating from college with a Bachelor of Science degree, I started to find out more about the learning process, the teaching practice, and how these could be applied to crystal ball reading. In my work toward my Master's degree in teaching, I learned that our current models for schooling were developed during the industrial era. With factories adding on new parts at each new stage, similar ideas for teaching students were adopted. Kids were assigned to grades, and at each new grade were subjected to new information that built upon the last grade. This process is called *scaffolding*, and will be used in this book. However, people are not factory parts, and everyone is not the same. Especially in a highly differentiated activity such as divination, where everyone's perceptions, interpretations, and even the beliefs that inform the two of those can be different, any classroom or book would be entirely insufficient.

As a result, to this day I still feel unable to successfully teach a "Crystal Ball 101"–style class with an entire room full of students, preferring instead that each of my students work at his or her own pace. Though I've published many smaller articles about spiritual development, this is my first adventure into the book-publishing world, and with its success I hope many others will follow. It is my hope that this book will be the next evolution in my teaching of this craft, and that it will initiate a whole new learning adventure in individual students all over the world. Thank you for being a part of my story about how I got started reading and teaching crystalomancy for beginners.

What Is a Crystal Ball?

Crystal gazing is the art of looking into a crystal ball to receive perceptions of the past, present, and future. Fortunetelling using a crystal ball, or crystalomancy, offers an opportunity to develop your divination skills to their natural limits with a tool that allows for easy transfer to other methods. The crystal ball itself is a pure crystal sphere, of any size, usually translucent and made of quartz. Crystal ball gazing can be a form of *scrying*, the practice by which literal or symbolic images are seen that are believed to have meaning and purpose. I chose the crystal ball as the subject for this book because I do believe scrying to be the best way to train natural intuitive abilities as they pop up, since it allows the most freedom of perception and the best way to get to know your own inner self through a divination tool. I also believe the crystal ball to be the best scrying tool for beginners, since it allows you to train yourself to scry with any tool, while giving possible added benefits of the properties of the crystal itself.

There are those who use the crystal ball without scrying. For this use, the crystal is used as a focal point to clear the mind for meditation, so that the information can be revealed through other means. This can be presented through the other senses, or simply arise as an understanding.

How Do You Scry with a Crystal Ball?

There are many who will find the systems of quiet receptivity and symbolic analysis in this book to be useful, including the divination beginner wishing to expand his or her repertoire of tools, or the natural psychic who can't seem to "turn off" visions or other purposeful perceptions and is desperately seeking a focus. This book does not pretend to be complete, and after reading it, you will not be guaranteed the ability to start your own fortunetelling business. No book can or should be the only resource for that, and I am still a staunch proponent of apprenticeships for that goal, but with this book you can expect guidance for beginning a personal practice of meditation and reading a crystal ball for yourself and others, if desired.

I began scrying naturally from my earliest childhood memories. As a rockhound child, picking up every quartz stone and frequenting gem shows with my parents, the use of small crystal spheres was an extension to this everyday practice. My parents were very encouraging of all my imaginative and spiritual pursuits, and my mother also practices divination. At the age of eighteen, I began selling readings professionally, using many different methods of divination—but scrying remains one of my favorites due to the unlimited freedom of what can be seen in the crystal ball. I currently have a large and growing client base, and I can't imagine not being a fortuneteller or not reading the crystal ball. I hope that others will share in the joy of my modern revival of this ancient art.

You, as the reader of this book, should have equal doses of faith and doubt. Expect to create a new language of symbols that may be partly a psychological science, and partly in the flexible realm of spirit and an evolving mythology. Along the way, mistakes and changes can be made, and that is okay. As Joseph Campbell wrote in his book *Myths to Live By*: "What would the meaning be of the word 'truth' to a modern scientist? Surely not the meaning it would have for a mystic! For the really great and essential fact about the scientific revolution—the most wonderful and challenging fact—is that science does not and cannot pretend to be 'true' in any absolute sense. It does not and cannot pretend to be final. It is a tentative organization of mere 'working hypotheses.'"[1]

History

The availability of other scrying media, such as fire and dark bowls filled with water, probably means that this practice predated the use of the crystal ball as a tool. Today, these older tools are still used, along with others. Scrying mirrors used in ceremonial magic are still used, and have

---

1. Campbell, *Myths to Live By*, 17.

found their way into modern folklore with ghost stories featuring mirrors and the fabled "Bloody Mary" appearing to frightened adolescents under specific circumstances such as Halloween, darkness, and the chanting of her name. Those with modern-day connections with Picts sometimes use a *keek-stane,* a darkened piece of convex glass set into a box or base.

The first users of crystals for divination were certainly religious. This early usage is attributed to the Druids, as early as 2000 BCE. Later, Scottish Highlanders used natural beryl for divination, valuing it for its transparent quality and replacing the beryl with more transparent crystals whenever possible. History and myth blur in medieval literature, where one finds crystal ball use by everyone from wizards to the Romani people.

Crystal balls have been used for séances since at least the eighteenth century. The setup of a traditional séance often used multiple family members around a table, holding hands or placing hands on the table with the little fingers touching, which allowed overwhelmed participants to pull away and reconnect with ease. A historical séance procedure compiled by Dr. Mark Mirabello, of Shawnee State University, suggests ritual objects similar to those that might be found in other Western magic circles, including a bell, rock salt, and a steel knife.[2] And a lily on the west side of the bowl, along with candles to the bowl's north and south.

---

2. See Mark Mirabello, PhD, "A Séance Procedure." PDF available online at http://www.markmirabello.com/seacuteance-procedure.html.

Later Christian influences to the largely Greek procedure included a Bible open to 1 Samuel, chapter 28, with a quartz crystal resting upon it. Incidentally, the Bible refers to crystal balls as *shewstones*. In Christian séances, having five people at the table was avoided, as it was believed that number of people would remind spirits too much of the five wounds that killed Christ.

If both meditation and scrying can be done with other, easier-to-obtain tools, why has the use of a crystal sphere persisted? Why did the Scottish Highlanders, who had an abundance of clear water, seek out the most transparent beryl that they could possibly obtain?

This book will lead you through the process of understanding not only what a crystal ball is and how to choose your own, but also the process of beginning to use the crystal ball to answer questions about love, money, and more. Step-by-step instructions will tell you what to look for and how to think about what you see. As you develop your skills with meditation, you will be guided to handle tricky interpretations with increasing ease—and even read for others, if that is your eventual goal.

Dive in to learn more about the ancient art of crystal ball reading and how it can help you.

one

How to Choose a Crystal Ball

A natural quartz crystal ball was once stolen from my person, a situation that makes me greatly concerned for the physical well-being of the thief and her family. (Be careful about buying a crystal from a pawn shop, as you never know what baggage it may bring home with you.) But it did cause my peers to rally around me to help me replace the lost divination tool, since they knew that this was how I made my living. I actually got wonderful results out of this bad situation, as I received two replacements—one the same size as the stolen sphere and one even larger.

The first replacement was the same size as the original and came from my spiritual teacher, Elder, and High

Priestess. She had actually ordered several quartz spheres of that size from an online gemstone retailer prior to the theft, and I remember she had me come out to her car and choose which one I would like to have. As I lifted each one to the light, I asked each one which was right for me and looked for the answer. In one of them I perceived the letters in my name presented in order inside the crystal ball, as if it were spelling my name, so it was quite clear that was the one for me. I blessed it during our ritual that night and have used it ever since.

My second replacement came from my mother, who went to a gem shop. The gem-shop owner, upon being asked for a crystal ball, erroneously pointed my mother at first to some impressively large glass spheres. My mother politely explained that she was looking for real crystals, and was shown to the natural quartz spheres. As the shop owner was not familiar with crystal ball reading at all, she began to show my mother the largest crystal spheres, as those are the most expensive. However, even though my mother was prepared to buy me the biggest crystal in the place, if that was the right one, she could tell that many of the very largest crystals were unsuitable, having not enough natural inclusions to catch the light. The shop owner must have been disappointed to see her pass by an enormous and nearly flawless crystal to choose a slightly smaller one with more imperfections.

How My Crystals Came into My Life

Scrying in many objects was a personal spiritual practice for as long as I can remember, but even I was nervous about procuring my first actual crystal ball. After all, a real piece of crystal is quite the financial investment for a child, even one who was spoiled with a large allowance. I had also heard a rumor from tarot-reading friends that a deck of cards should not be bought, but should be given to you. Now, that isn't necessarily true, but I wondered at the time if it would apply to crystal balls as well, and whether I could manipulate this bit of lore in order to get myself a free crystal ball.

I needn't have worried, because my Aunt Sue is incredibly supportive of my divination arts, requesting readings herself at times, and also loves to buy me trinkets for no reason at all. And so, my first crystal ball was a small one, mounted in a necklace, toward which I merely had to point my finger and show the slightest interest to my aunt before she rushed to purchase it for me. I didn't even have to begin my well-rehearsed story about why it was important. I also rationalized to myself that, if it somehow didn't work, I could simply wear it as a piece of jewelry. Of course, it did work just fine, and I still use it to this day, as a way to inconspicuously carry around a crystal ball.

My mother has also been a professional fortuneteller, and although she is retired now, she still offers her talents at fundraisers and for family and friends. She has purchased several crystal balls for me, and she always has an eye for those that fit the right specifications. The two of us love to talk shop about performing readings, and we even had a chance to work side by side on a cruise to the Bahamas with a "psychics on the sea" theme!

Once I started using my first crystal ball, I was hooked. Surely, some of my initial motivations for trying it out had to do with simply being involved in this ancient art that was recognized in a very widespread way, and yet so mysterious to all involved. Once I tried it out, I was surprised at how easy it was. I had imagined squinting my eyes at a clear sphere and giving up after not being able to make out a thing. But as the images and symbols were easily found in the rainbows and shiny sparkles inside even my tiny crystal ball, I was hungry for more. I must admit, thought, that my desire for additional and larger crystals was also because it might be more impressive than gazing into a tiny marble.

My next crystal ball came to me as a birthday present from a friend and client, who knew of my interest in divination of all sorts. It was small also, one and a half inches in diameter, but was wonderful for travel. It came in a small, velvet bag, and is still the crystal I bring with me when going on a trip by car or plane, since it is unlikely to get broken when wedged deep in my clothing bag. I do choose to use this slightly larger crystal ball over my necklace when traveling, when I don't have to be discreet—not because it is more effective, but simply because it is easier to allow light into a larger crystal while holding it, since your fingers don't block off a large percentage of the surface area. The same friend and client later gave me an amethyst crystal sphere of the same size that, while good for healing readings, I do not often use, because the purple hue can obscure some of the other colors that might come through in my readings.

My next steps up in crystal collection and size were crystal spheres about three inches in diameter, given to me by my mother and my spiritual teacher. I find this size to be ideal for most cases, because it is large enough that there are many small imperfections inside to examine and small enough that it fits into the palm of one hand to be turned easily and exposed to the light. I find this size and larger is the size for which I most often reach. It can also fairly easily travel in a purse, though one has to be careful not to knock the bag against anything.

My largest crystal ball, about four inches in diameter, is the one I use at home. Its size is impressive, so I certainly bring it to events at which I will be on camera, but I do worry about dropping or breaking it in transit due to the fact that it must be handled with two hands and is somewhat more heavy. At any rate, regardless of size, any crystal ball has advantages over more organized divination systems due to the ease of scrying and the freedom and diversity of what can be seen.

What to Look for

Before you select your first crystal ball, it is important to decide for what purpose you would like to use it. If you intend to attempt to see visions in it at all, transparency is key. Thus, for your first crystal, the best choice may be a natural quartz crystal sphere. You're looking for a sphere that overall is so clear that, when holding it in your hand, you should be able to clearly see the color of your fingers. However, an entirely clear ball is not what you want. Look for small "inclusions," or tiny flaws within the crystal that will look like flat, rainbow, three-dimensional effects. Clear, lead crystal is unsuitable due to its lack of flaws. The ideal crystal ball will have countless inclusions but be otherwise clear. Some cloudiness is okay, but not so much that it obscures your inclusions.

If you are absolutely sure that you do not want to attempt to see visions in the crystal and only wish to use it for meditative and trance purposes, then you have a lot more freedom and can choose an opaque crystal, transparent or translucent. I find that, for this purpose, a more shiny crystal of a very consistent hue can be best. The shine of the crystal can create optical illusions that allow you to better soften your focus, and a lack of color variation does not tempt your mind to be distracted by perceived shapes.

As for the size of your crystal ball, size is truly not the most important factor. I used to joke when I was first getting into crystal ball reading, upon discovering the expense of large, quartz spheres, that I wanted to start a rumor that the smaller the crystal ball was, the more accurate it was. This has not proven to be true in my experience. At the time of this writing, my smallest quartz crystal sphere is one centimeter in diameter and my largest crystal sphere is ten (about four inches). I switch sizes between readings without any further thought than travel considerations.

Beyond clear or white quartz, there are a myriad of gemstones that can be used, as long as they can be made to conform to a spherical shape. There are correspondences that can be used for many purposes, and I encourage you to experiment. A reader might choose to use his or her birthstone, or even of the month in which the reading is taking place.

Here are some examples of stones or colors that can be used. For Aries readers, or for the month of March, a carnelian sphere or any red crystal can be used. Aries was also the god of war, so readings or meditations over conflicts and anger or impulsive actions may be aided. Mars is also associated with the color red and with Aries. Tuesday, once called *Tyr's Day*, can be the most auspicious time to work with these correspondences.

For Taurus readers, carnelian, which is related to the month of April, can also be a useful gemstone. However, any stone of the color indigo can also work well. Gemini or the month of May can be associated with topaz, which can come in many hues, so if you can find one that is purple, that would be best. Cancer or the month of June corresponds with the gemstone chalcedony, or any crystal that is maroon in color. Readings for Leo or July would find Jasper or the color purple to be most auspicious. Virgo or August can use emerald, or any slate-gray gemstone. Libra or September can make use of the fabled beryl, or a stone of the color blue. Scorpio or October has the amethyst crystal ball, or any brown crystal sphere. Sagittarius or November works best with the hyacinth stone or any yellow crystal.

Capricorn or December can use the chrysoprase gemstone or a black crystal. Aquarius or January works well with any sky blue crystal sphere, and Pisces or February can use a sapphire sphere or any tan-colored stone.

No matter what is going on in the world, love is always foremost on the minds of many, so I'd recommend a green crystal ball for love questions. If the questions have more to do with career, a black stone is good for one with a strong sense of organization—but if you have to take the lead, a blue one may work better. Health readings can be done with purple crystals. I know a healer who uses an amethyst crystal ball for all of her health readings, as was advised by author and healer Uma Silbey in her book *Crystal Ball Gazing*. As for those questions that deal with the dead, I still have best luck with white or clear crystals, which are also associated with the moon.

You may wonder about the convention of the spherical crystal. While people do use gazing crystals of all shapes for meditation and scrying, this obviously departs from the practice of crystal ball reading. I do believe that the sphere is the best shape for scrying and meditation, because it allows you to rotate the crystal in your hands freely while keeping the distance from the surface to the occlusions within the crystal ball relatively the same. You also have the added benefit of allowing the optical illusion of the images in the room being projected upside down to your eye by the lens effect of the light refracting, in order to help your visual focus and your mental trance. If you gaze into any convex lens, such as the side of a sphere facing toward you,

you will see your own reflection upside down. If you gaze into any concave lens, such as the surface of the sphere farthest away from you if you look through the crystal ball, light can create an image to form just in front of the lens.

Every once in a while, some enterprising person comes up with another shape of crystal or another material that they proclaim is best for scrying. This is similar to diamond jewelry retailers who come up with their own patented diamond cut. The funny thing about that is that the round diamond cut is mathematically the best for the properties of any diamond to display the diamond's light refraction to the human eye. For this reason, all diamond certifications have to be performed on round-cut diamonds, and the round cut has endured through many a patented fad cut. Likewise, the sphere-cut shape of a crystal presents its ideal properties for scrying.

What to Avoid

My one request is that you please don't use just a glass sphere. Though I'm not knocking any other scrying tool, glass spheres cannot, by definition, be used for crystal ball gazing. Even though they can be very impressive, as cheap ones can be purchased that are great in size, such spheres diverge away from crystal ball use into another form of scrying, and if you are to experiment with this form of divination, I'd ask you to stay true to the tool. The reason that the use of glass spheres is a bit of a pet peeve of mine is because, as a crystal ball reader, you are an ambassador for this enduring art—and family, friends, or clients who see you use glass spheres and mistake it for crystal ball reading may develop misconceptions. I also think that going for size over possible substance is choosing theatricality over practicality, which isn't the purpose of this book.

Where to Find Your Crystal Ball

This is not something that you should order from a catalog or online, if at all possible. However, there is something to be said about just starting as soon as possible with the materials at hand and buying a better version later. Visit a local metaphysical bookstore or gem shop and ask about what you want. Just remember that the old standby is a quartz crystal with the properties that are outlined in this chapter for scrying. Move to the correct section of the store and pay attention to what feelings draw or repel you. If you've made good use of your intuition in the past, hold each stone in your hands before purchase and use your gut feeling to select the one that is right for you.

How to Care for It and Store It

Once you've selected your crystal or crystals, there is no one set of instructions for their proper care and feeding. I've not yet broken a crystal ball, myself (knock on wood), but due to the nature of the inclusions being of a different density than the rest of your crystal ball, it is important to avoid exposing your crystal ball to extreme temperatures or physical trauma. If you do plan to use your crystal ball in a spiritual context, you can bless it through your own spiritual tradition. I blessed mine in a magical circle during an appropriate time. If you have a regular space that you can use for meditation and trance work, your crystal ball can be placed there on a stand. I keep mine on a family altar, to which my husband adds objects that we find have spiritual meaning to us.

The material of the stand does not matter too much, although some magic circles avoid the use of silver, as that is reserved for the Goddess, or the use of iron, as that is believed to ward off some fairies. I have stands made of plastic and stands made of wood. It is important that the stands not be distracting, so there should not be carvings or decorations on the stand that distract your eye from the crystal.

Many lighted stands are available for purchase that make the crystal ball look quite lovely. I even own one of those with a light that changes colors. I bring it with me to fairs and festivals so that passersby will be drawn to the beauty of the shifting colored light as it shines up through the crystal ball on my table. Though you are welcome to use such lighted stands when your crystal ball is just on display for ornamentation, I do not find them to be at all useful during reading, and I do turn mine off, probably quite anticlimactically, when a client is ready for a reading. One that changes colors would be distracting from trance work and would mask any colors that emerge through your own perception of the crystal's qualities.

I even find that just a white lighted stand is not as good as using external overhead lighting, candles, or natural light.

The harsh glare can tend to obscure the natural inclusions for me. Ideal lighting for me while scrying is indirect sunlight or a full-spectrum overhead light, while the best lighting for me for simple meditation is candlelight, just to help me get into a relaxed mood.

One last note about lighting is to avoid direct sunlight when working with your crystal ball outdoors. From personal experience, I can tell you that a crystal ball in direct sunlight acts like a magnifying glass burning ants, except that it refracts unpredictably within the natural crystal to allow the focused heat to beam out at a random location. I would never have thought of this until I had a photo shoot with a crystal ball in the sunlight and noticed a burning sensation on my hand as I held the crystal. Beware of starting a fire. It turns out that in addition to metaphorical *chi,* or "energy"—which is the phenomenon that connects the universe and manifests love, life, and change—you must be aware of how very real radiant energy reacts within your crystal.

Note that you can own several crystal balls for different purposes. You can switch freely between them, even during one reading. Some practitioners are careful to thank their crystal ball, as if it were a person, before switching to another in order to explain to the crystal ball that it will be asked for help again in the future. This anthropomorphism may help you feel as though you're developing a rapport with your crystals, but it can also be omitted if you feel that it is silly.

Be aware, though, that some practitioners believe that their tools take on very real personalities, and can be offended in a way that affects their use. It is a well-known legend that stolen divination tools can tend to create negative effects in the lives of the thieves. I know a reader who has a crystal for each reading topic she does, and rather than choosing a crystal for each purpose, she believes that the crystals seemed to select themselves as one began giving greater detail for her during love readings and one seemed to give more information during readings about conflict. If you will be using your crystal ball to attempt to speak with the dead, then you should know that in many traditional religions, such as that of the Yoruba people, it is believed that ancestors can get in the way of proper divination, and indeed many other aspects of life, if not properly honored and respected. *Animism*, which can include the thought that even crystals have souls, is a part of many traditional Native American religions.

It is proper etiquette not to touch the divination tools of another person, something that can certainly be applicable for a crystal ball, and not only for the obvious reason that somebody could drop and break it or smudge it. If you believe in the life energy of chi (and even if you don't), the possibility exists that someone could purposely or accidentally ground the carefully developed, nurtured, and stored chi that is within your crystal ball. One might also rub off personal chi that you do not want inside your crystal ball, including emotional baggage or ill intent. Foreign chi has the potential to alter the way your crystal ball works, if only very slightly, which can slow your own learning time as you work to develop a personal rapport with your specific crystal ball.

On the other hand, there may be some benefits to other people handling your crystal ball if you choose to read for other people. The chi that rubs off onto the crystal from the person for whom you are reading may be able to better allow symbolism that is significant to them to come through. Every person who handles your crystal ball might add their own chi and symbolism to it, expanding its repertoire and also your own. Thus, the best solution for you to reap these benefits may be for you to have at least two crystal balls, one that you can allow others to handle and the other that is off limits. I would suggest that the larger and more expensive of the two be the one that only you are allowed to touch.

If you must store your crystal ball out of sight, you can keep it wrapped in black cloth or in a black bag, as is traditional for many divination tools. During transit, I carry mine in a padded box. In case you're wondering: yes, I have successfully taken a crystal ball in my carry-on luggage when traveling by plane. At one point, when my carry-on was scanned by the x-ray machine, a curious airport official did take my crystal ball out of my bag and ask me what it was, followed by his taking out my tarot cards and sorting through them, one by one, to make sure that I hadn't stashed anything nefarious among them. My other divination tools must have been less threatening, as they were left undisturbed.

You may wear your crystal ball, if it is a small one. In fact, my smallest crystal ball, the one that is just a centimeter in diameter, is mounted as a pendant, wrapped in a silver claw loosely so that the crystal can still freely move within the claw. If you do choose to wear your crystal ball, make sure that the mounting of it does not interfere with lighting, visibility, or the ability for the crystal to rotate. That said, wearing your crystal can be a great idea. Not only is it a beautiful conversation piece, but the properties of the gemstone—protective, healing, or otherwise—may also be imparted to you. Moreover, you have the added benefit of always having your crystal ball with you, should you have a need to meditate or scry with it.

Before you begin to meditate or scry with your crystal ball, you may wish to do some preparation of it. This has two benefits. One, if you believe in chi, is to clear it of any negative chi and imbue it with the proper chi aligned with your intentions. The other benefit is purely psychological. That is, if you allow yourself to only use the crystal ball with the intent to depart from everyday life, it will more easily allow you to get into that mind state. So, finding ways to designate your crystal as anything but ordinary can help engender that respect for your purpose.

Cleansing or clearing is the most important step in this process. Similar to what I described in the story at the beginning of this chapter, it is possible that some very negative chi may have come along with your crystal. If you're not familiar with working with chi, you can cleanse your crystal physically with water, and then bury it in a box full of salt for a moon cycle to achieve good effect. If you are already familiar with visualization techniques and prayer, you can visualize light and color from your crystal's potentially sordid past flowing harmlessly out of the crystal and into the earth, praying for it to go away and be converted by the earth into more positive stuff.

To consecrate or charge the crystal ball to your purpose, you can also use prayer and visualization—this time praying for it to help you receive the messages you need to get, and visualizing color and light flowing up from the earth and into your crystal ball, representing the power you will require. If you are unfamiliar with working with chi, your crutch for charging your crystal ball can be sleeping with it underneath your pillow, if possible, for a moon cycle, or allowing it to be exposed to full moonlight. You can also touch it to representations of the four elements—incense for air, water, fire, and salt for earth—to help bless it.

two

How to Read a
Crystal Ball

A new client requested a sitting with a professional psychic, a friend and colleague of mine who works under the name of Azzrian Visions. Azzrian usually prefers to conduct her readings without divination tools, relying instead on what she believes are her guides, spirits she feels are always with her. That works well for most of her clients, who are regulars to the psychic industry and many of whom have grown weary and skeptical of tarot readings, a mainstay in the current landscape of practices.

This time, however, Azzrian had many tools available. She sat in her home deep in meditation. The lights were low, allowing the sunlight to slip through the window, highlighting the blue and lavender shades of the room. Her altar sat atop a natural wood table, handed down to her from her family. Atop it were various photographs of her ancestors, as well as herbs and oils giving off a rich scent. For this reading with this client, Azzrian was drawn to use her crystal ball.

When Azzrian uses a crystal ball, she doesn't always literally see things inside it. Instead, she likens her sense more to "listening" to a vibration. It's as if she can hear a frequency mentally, and whether it is higher or lower tells her the answer to a question she is asking. She took great care in asking her crystal questions for her client, believing that interpretation of the answers is the most difficult part of reading with any tool. Suddenly, quite unexpectedly, she connected with a dead person whom the client had loved. Azzrian carefully let the client know, "I have a spirit with us that wants to come through." She added that it was the spirit of the client's father.

The details flowed quickly and easily. She named the exact make of his favorite car, which he had hung onto doggedly throughout his life, long after it had ceased to run. She knew that he had made his own hearing aid, having been unsatisfied with the kinds you could buy. As the messages continued to emerge from the crystal, Azzrian saw her client fill with joy, knowing for certain that her father was with them in that moment.

How I Learned to Read the Crystal Ball

As a small child, I may not have had the healthy dose of skepticism that keeps me from making so many mistakes now, but I did have complete freedom from self-doubt, a fear of being foolish, and inhibitions. I also had the natural tendency to be imaginative and make connections. These skills lent themselves as easily to divination as they did to flights of fancy. If I thought I saw a rock by a stream in my bowl of cereal in the morning, I would gladly go down to the neighborhood stream to fetch a similar rock without concern about why my corn flakes would tell me to do so, or whether I was being downright crazy. Much of this impulsiveness and exploratory sense of wonder stays with me today.

As a beginner first looking into a crystal ball, I was doubtful that I would be able to see a television-like image projected onto the surface of the crystal ball, as I had seen in cartoons and kids' shows. It is a good thing, too, because I wasn't disappointed. Rather, I was pleasantly surprised that the crystal ball wasn't necessarily an empty, clear, sphere-like glass. There were many entertaining natural deformations within my crystal that sparkled and refracted light to shine rainbows back to my eyes.

Recognizing shapes was easy to me. I would see, for example, a tiny imperfection in the crystal that looked like it was shaped just like a heart. I did not need to soften my focus, or even stretch my imagination too hard, as the human mind is good at picking out and recognizing shapes. Some images, like the heart, were easy symbols to recognize and attribute directly to a concept like love. But others, like a man wearing a hat, seemed to be confusing and potentially meaningless at first. I questioned whether all of these symbols had meanings for them, or whether some should be dismissed at first, but over time I discovered that puzzling out the meanings of each symbol has great value, even if they may seem like nonsensical stretches of the imagination when you first view them.

As a distractible and hyperactive kid, I found the crystal ball and scrying in general to be an easy choice over other forms of divination such as tarot cards, since I was immediately turned off by the idea of needing to read a long book about how to proceed and memorizing a list of somebody else's symbols. With a crystal ball, I could simply look in and allow the crystal and my own mind to teach me what I needed to know and show me what I needed to see. I could talk with others about their own experiences with scrying, since I did not have access to books about crystal gazing at the time; I was not dismissed to the library, as I might have been with questions about more popular forms of divination that have been frequently analyzed in a scholarly way.

This same freedom from a limited list of symbols is what drew me over and over again to the crystal ball and scrying as an adult. When I would have an issue, concern, or fear, I needn't be constrained to burying my head in a book and reaching to understand how a paragraph applied to my life. Instead, if I was worried about how a friend was doing, I could actually see her in the crystal ball, doing fine, or I would be shown a happy symbol to which I would immediately react with emotional relief.

The instant gratification factor was key, but it did make me wonder in the beginning if I was sacrificing accuracy for ease of use with the crystal ball. After all, there were so many forms of divination to which I had already been exposed. Early on, I began to wonder just which one was the very best. As an experienced reader now, I choose the tool based on the job at hand. Just as a hammer and a saw can both be used on wood, the crystal ball is one of several divination tools that can be used upon a question to be answered.

Accuracy and precision are separate concepts. Imagine a bull's-eye target, at which you are to shoot many arrows. If the arrows were clustered together in a tight group a little up and to the right of the bull's-eye, that would demonstrate precision but not accuracy. If the arrows were generally in and around the bull's-eye evenly, but spread apart with few or no outliers, that would show accuracy but not precision. Ideally, you want all of those arrows clustered together in a tight grouping in the dead center of the bull's-eye. That is both precision *and* accuracy.

Accuracy, by and large, appears to be a function of you as a reader. Interpretation is like learning a new language, and the more you practice with it, the fewer mistakes you will make. But just as you can misspeak or mess up anything in your life, you can still make mistakes with crystal ball reading. Precision is the aspect that is somewhat influenced by your divination tool and with the way in which you use your divination tool.

For example, a skilled palmist can be very accurate, but the lines in the palm aren't going to show me the hair color of a client's future husband, or the letters in his name, so I would turn to the crystal ball for detailed descriptions. An experienced pendulum dowser may accurately divine a "yes" or "no" to a question about whether a marriage proposal is coming soon, but a crystal ball reading on the marriage might show numbers in the date as well, and may also reveal symbols that show how you could move the date up so that it is sooner. Tarot cards might show you if your sister's husband is cheating on her, but you can't see names in the cards, so if you also wanted to know letters in the name of the other woman, again I might suggest turning to the crystal ball.

The greatest questions I asked myself when I was a beginner with the crystal ball was how it worked so well. Who guides my viewfinder to take the right snapshot? Is it intelligent design? Who can say? Self-knowledge is one thing, but I was amazed at the accuracy I could have reading for strangers with my crystal ball, even when at a distance over the telephone or the Internet. I decided from my long-distance experiences with no feedback from others that I couldn't simply just be "sucking" information out of my own chi or the chi of a person sitting in front of me.

"As above, so below": These words, which have been attributed to an ancient writer named Hermes Trismegistus, struck a chord with my scientific, college-educated mind as well as my spiritual self. These four words express the theory that the universe is full of repeating yet chaotic patterns. If you examine very closely the tiny curl of a fractal pattern, it looks the same as the bigger picture. In the same ways, the grand dance of the stars above are thought to mirror our miniscule actions here on earth through the practice of astrology. And what is seen within a crystal ball can be representative of what is happening on a much larger scale in the life of another person.

With this amazing power to view the entire universe in a crystal sphere in the palm of my hand, I also realized that I still didn't know everything. Though I hoped, and still hope, that the crystal ball is unlimited, I know that my own ability to think things through is only human. My dreams of using psychic powers to see all that might ever happen to me vanished, and I began to feel annoyed when friends and strangers assumed that I knew everything as well. This was especially embarrassing to me when I was mugged for my crystal ball while I performed readings at a public fair in Seattle.

Most people would laugh at a headline about a crystal ball reader being robbed and ask, "Shouldn't she have seen that coming?" Ironically, perceptive though I am, I can also be rather disconnected from the real world at times, and am certainly never omniscient nor omnipotent. While in a trance state, I can be slow to react to emergency situations should they arise, or not mentally aware enough to make sure that everything is business as usual. That's why I now always ask for payment before I begin a professional reading, after letting too many clients walk away with both of us forgetting. A colleague of mine places a sign behind her that reads: "Your psychic is in a very special headspace. Please do not forget to pay her!"

I've always had my head in the clouds, and with an active imagination, scrying was everywhere in my life—and that only increased as the years went on. Ironically, the crystal ball became a valuable tool for me to contain what I was seeing, rather than drawing it out. If I had a terrifying dream or a waking vision of a ghost, I could grab the crystal ball and use it as a safe place to explore that imagery, while actively working to block it out of the rest of my life in order to keep me operating in consensus reality with everyone else.

After the death of my father, this was especially helpful to me. His presence was immediately everywhere in my life, and I was just as concerned about the spirit world consuming me as he was about scaring me, or making me insane. But when I requested that he appear in my dreams or in my crystal ball, it was not only an easy way to communicate but also a good way to set boundaries, especially after the appearance of his ghost terrified a housesitter. The advantage of crystal ball reading over other forms of divination is incredible, since I was actually able to see my deceased loved one again. In my experience, comparing tarot cards to the crystal ball in this context is like comparing your loved one flashing Morse code over a lake with a flashlight to having a video conference call with him.

Establish Your Main Symbol

I will outline steps you can take to get comfortable with a ritual or routine for scrying with your crystal ball and finding at least one main symbol. Experienced crystal ball readers easily jump from one symbol to another, but as a beginner it can be easier to keep it simple in order not to feel overwhelmed by a flood of symbols or disappointed when you can't manage more than a single one.

As a beginner, I learned that some days and times are better for certain purposes. The best times of year for any form of divination are Beltane, May 1st; and Samhain, October 31st. It is believed that these are the times of the year when the veil between the worlds is at its thinnest. Likewise, the full moon is an especially good time for scrying. Check an almanac or ephemeris for the exact time of the full moon in your area and notice how different you feel if you practice before or after the full moon. This doesn't necessarily mean that you can only scry once per month. The more correspondences with which you can align, the more auspicious your readings may be, but I've used divination on every day of the year. The waxing moon can be a good time for advice on starting and growing projects, and the waning moon can be good for seeking guidance on cutting away and diminishing things that no longer serve you.

The days of the week have their proper correspondences as well. Monday is *Moon Day*, and is good for questions about cycles, magic, fears, or women. *Tyr's Day*, or Tuesday, is associated with Mars and is good for conflicts, sports, anger, or action. *Woden's Day*, Wednesday, is for Mercury, a day for healing, communications, study, travel, and situations that might involve trickery. *Thor's Day*, or Thursday, is associated with Jupiter, for situations that involve leadership, money, or legal matters. *Freya Day*, Friday, is for Venus, and is best suited for questions about love, one's social life, and generosity. *Saturn Day*, or Saturday, can be the day for order, getting rid of bad things, and for employment and work. *Sun Day* can be good for nurturing power, recognition, and growth.

Even the hour of the day can be relevant for your scrying purposes. The first planetary hour of each day always matches the planet of the day. So sunrise on Sunday is the hour of the Sun. The planetary hours march onward in this order repeatedly: Sun, Venus, Mercury, Moon, Saturn, Jupiter, Mars. The next day resets the repeating cycle.

So, if you were going to establish your main symbol at the absolutely perfect time for love, it would be in the hour of Venus, on a Friday, during the full moon on Beltane, but if you can hit any of these correspondences at all it may help. If you are scrying in order to find out how best to get over a bad divorce, the perfect time might be in the hour of Saturn on a Saturday during a full moon on Samhain. There are some times that can get in the way of scrying. The dark moon can be a time of rest, as well as when the moon is void of course. Mercury retrograde won't hurt the scrying itself, but it might mess up your ability to communicate clearly if you are trying to communicate the results to someone else.

As you follow the steps here at the time when you feel ready, keep in mind that there is no one ritual that people throughout the world use for scrying with the crystal ball. I will provide some example steps that you can use, letting you know which are vital for the practice so that you can customize your own practices if you wish. You may find that your ritual becomes more simple or more elaborate as you become more experienced.

The steps that follow are just an overview, which I'm providing here in a succinct form so that you can get started right away. I will, however, be describing the process in greater detail throughout the book.

Step 1: Construct Your Questions

In the beginning, we're going to try to keep as much intellectual analysis out of the actual trance scrying as possible, but with experience you may find these steps blend together. Your desire to scry with the crystal ball was probably prompted by a question that needed to be answered. Use it as an aid to help you move toward your desired options. So instead of asking "Will I?" or "Will it?" try to develop a road map for how to get there by asking, "What should I do in order to achieve my outcome?"

For example, instead of asking, "Will my boyfriend ask me to marry him next year?" or "Will I get a job soon?" you could ask, "What should I do in order to improve the chances that my boyfriend will ask me to marry him next year?" or "What should I be thinking about or changing in my life in order to get a job soon?"

Ask questions about what your concern, focus, or actions should be. Write them down in a notebook for use during your reading. For your first reading, I'd suggest condensing them all into one overarching question that you can explore very thoroughly.

And what if you don't know what you want? Hey, it's great that you're being honest with yourself. But just because you haven't made a decision yet doesn't mean somebody else is going to make it for you. Not knowing what will happen is no excuse to bust out the "Will it happen?" questions. Instead, you can use the reading to help you with the process itself: "What should I be thinking about as I make my decision about . . . ?" Or, conversely, you could use the crystal ball to help play out a scenario to make your decision: "What would I need to be concerned with if I chose this course of action?" Exploring scenarios, and deciding which scenario is best, is better than imagining we live in a world in which events occur only as a result of somebody else's decisions.

Step 2: Define Your Space

You'll need to be in a place with few distractions where you won't be disturbed. Many people find that other actions to declare a sacred space help their readings. If you are familiar with circle-casting techniques, you can use your own. Defining the space in which you read as a circle can help you keep all of the spirits or chi that you want close to you, so that they don't dissipate before you've achieved your purpose. It also allows you to keep that area mentally or spiritually clean of all distractions, seen and unseen. You can draw a literal circle with salt, flour, or a length of rope. You can also visualize a circle in your mind as you create it.

Your circle should be a microcosm that symbolically reflects the universe out of which you plan to retrieve answers to your questions. Thus, within it, you can have representations of the four elements, which often include incense for the direction of east and the element of air, a lit candle for fire in the south, water for west, and salt to represent earth in the north. It is beyond the scope of this book to explore the many ways in which your circle can be cleansed and built, so I will give an example of the quickest circle-casting I ever wrote, written in rhyme for a college friend to help her remember in what order she wanted to do things:

(Walk counterclockwise while holding a cup of water with a pinch of salt added to it.)

Now I cleanse the space for holy circle round

With every touch of water to the ground.

(Walk clockwise holding out your hand as a spiritual blade, or *athame*.)

Three times now the circle is cast

Spring forth from my blade and seal fast.

(Walk clockwise again, holding lit incense.)

Now so cleansed and sealed so tight
To keep the worldly out
I call for blessings of the Gods
Surround me all about!

Another ritual object that you may find helpful to have within your reach is a bell, to ring in order to acknowledge each of the four directions of the compass that make up the world around you. Bells have been used in many cultures to draw positive spirits near while scaring negative ones away. The sound can also help to calm and center your mind, as well as create a mental key that conditions you that it is time to work. If you do pray, this is a good time to address any deities and ask for blessings.

Step 3: Ground and Trance

This a step that I really must insist that you keep. If you are new to grounding, a more complete discussion of how to do it is in the next chapter.

Relax and focus on your breathing in order to sink into a trance state and attempt to see, feel, or understand a message, depending on which sense aids you best. Meditation is one good way to induce the trance that is necessary for many people to do crystal ball reading. If you are able to use more than one perception, allow yourself to switch between them for each question, if comfortable, or choose just one for each reading while you practice. The practice of asking whether it is right to begin a divination session and whether it is time to end the session is used in the Ifa divination practices, as well as in some séance processes. Before you begin to scry for your main symbol, you may wish to ask the crystal ball for permission to scry. To avoid the frustration of asking a question that cannot be answered in your present situation, ask if this is the right time and the right question. Wait for a "yes" or "no" indicator that seems correct to you. If a negative reaction is given, thank the crystal and use this as a meditation time. If a positive answer is given, it is time to begin to scry.

Step 4: View Your Main Symbol

Each of the senses can be used to view symbols with the crystal ball, including literally seeing the occlusions form shapes, similar to how clouds in the sky form shapes; visualizing pictures in your mind's eye; or even knowing the message in your head as a deep understanding. Since the lighting conditions, your frame of mind, and the angle at which the crystal ball is held are never quite identical, you see the occlusions appear to assume different shapes under different circumstances even during the same reading on the same day.

I always use the example "like clouds in the sky" with people, and that seems to make sense to them. Everyone can see shapes in clouds in the sky, shapes that are always in flux, even though the clouds look relatively similar.

The symbols in a crystal ball can be viewed with no particular structure, or you can use a system of constellations. As a beginner, there may be too much focus on what each symbol means. You're not building a sentence full of nouns and verbs, but a story full of characters. Learning how to weave the meanings together into a coherent story can be more challenging than the individual meanings themselves, so it is best to begin by limiting yourself to one main symbol as you learn this art, and to record it for later interpretation.

There is more information about how to do this step under the "What to Look for" heading a bit later in this chapter.

Step 5: Ground and Close Your Circle

Ground immediately after the scrying session. This part I cannot emphasize enough, as even if you do not outwardly find yourself experiencing headaches, dizziness, or other symptoms of being ungrounded, you may leave yourself open to bringing some of your scrying state back to your regular waking life, which can disorient you at the very least and can also lessen the effectiveness that comes with keeping your trance states and your waking states as completely separate as possible.

Just as good campers take down their camp carefully, leaving no trace behind in the wilderness, you must dismantle your circle in the same way. Begin by thanking any deities or entities that were called. Reel your circle back in by sweeping away, picking up, or rubbing out the edges in the same way that you laid them out. If you used the circle setup that was given here as an example, you might choose to walk counterclockwise with the water and incense again in order to repeat the spiritual cleansing that you did before your circle. Extinguish any candles at this point, and a very literal cleaning may be in order for the room in which you've set up this activity.

Step 6: Interpretation

Though this can be performed before you take down your circle, it shouldn't be performed before grounding when you are beginning. Once you are fully out of your trance, write down what you believe the initial meanings of the symbols you saw to mean and write them in a notebook to use as your own personal dictionary. You can come back to this later to see if your interpretations have changed.

If some of the symbols puzzle you, and their interpretations are unclear, make a note of this so that you can plan a meditation session for each of those symbols. This process may seem cumbersome, but it is best for setting you up to be fluent with your crystal. Later on, it may be easier for you to dip in and out of the trance state in order to convey the messages of what you experienced, but in the beginning you may need your wits about you for some of your interpretations. At the very least, you'll need to know how you're thinking about them. So you should clearly make notes to delineate when you are approaching the symbols with intellectual analysis and when you are approaching them with intuitive meditation. Both methods can be used for the best effect, eventually in tandem.

What to Look for

Before you get on a roll with practicing the flow of readings with your crystal ball, it is important to do some experimentation to find out how your own perception with the crystal ball is going to work. Each person's perceptions may vary greatly. Some people may see literal shapes and colors within the crystal ball. Others may not literally see visions, but instead visualize shapes and colors within the mind's eye. Still others may not visualize at all, but rather have another sense such as a literal or figurative "feeling," or discover understandings arising in the mind in the form of thoughts.

I personally see visions, prompted from what I imagine the shapes of the occlusions inside the crystal ball to look like. So, if I see a cloudy imperfection that looks like a man-shaped image, I might also see a whole lot more detail. Other people may not be so "lucky," but they can still see a man-shaped image that can have symbolic meaning.

Your interpretations and even your perceptions of the same occlusions may vary each time you use the same crystal ball. If a heart-shaped image looks complete versus broken or fuzzy, your interpretation may differ accordingly, or maybe at another angle the heart actually looks like the letter *V*; or, if observed upside down, it looks more like a mountain than a heart. This is the same as seeing shapes in tea leaves as well. Yes, they are always leaves, but the clumps of leaves look different each time.

Grab a crystal ball if you have one handy, and go ahead and find a specific fleck in it. Then, turn it around a lot in your hand before trying to find the same fleck again. I have trouble doing this. I think you'll find it just as difficult. Turning the crystal too quickly can even make it impossible for me to go back and further examine something I've just seen, so I recommend pausing the moment you see something and perhaps writing it down or sketching it.

Gaze into the crystal and experiment with what perceptions you can have of what is inside the crystal ball. Begin by examining the small flaws inside the crystal. If you selected the ideal crystal with many inclusions, they should be rainbow-colored and have varied shapes. Allow yourself to turn the crystal ball in your hands, stopping the turning motion when something catches your eye.

If you can see shapes in the clouds in the sky, you should be able to scry. Pretend that all of those tiny flaws inside your crystal are clouds and allow yourself to see shapes in them. Identify the objects you see in your mind, but be careful to release the thoughts to keep yourself in a trance state. If you are successful with this process, then you can count yourself among one of the visual scryers who is using literal images inside the crystal ball. If you are unable to make out anything with your attempts, then check to see if you're just naturally another type of perceiver.

If you were unsuccessful with this type of scrying, allow your eyes to relax and soften your focus on the crystal so that you are looking through it, as if gazing at something beyond. When you can relax into this, wait for mental images to appear. Don't force this to happen. Return to meditating if you find yourself attempting visualization. If you do begin to "see" inner images in your mind's eye, acknowledge and dismiss them. You can count yourself as one of the people who can figuratively see things in the crystal ball. If either of the above visual techniques didn't work for you, allow yourself to explore your other senses, as there are many successful readers who never use visual techniques with the crystal ball.

If neither visual technique was successful, keep that soft-focus view on the crystal and pay attention to your sense of touch. Does the sphere feel lighter at some times and heavier at others? Can you perceive a soft, fuzzy feeling at times? Feel for a change in temperature, texture, and pressure. Far from being any less effective or legitimate than the visual methods, the sense of touch is a very common way that people perceive the universe's life energy, or chi.

You can even pay attention to other senses. During a trance state, it is not crazy to hear voices. As your brain dips into the alpha-wave state associated with the restful state before sleep, healthy people can naturally perceive sounds that aren't there. Even scent and taste might come alive during your trance work with the crystal. My mother smells my dead father's cigarette smoke whenever his spirit is near her.

If none of the senses with which you are familiar worked for you, you may have come into the tricky world of trying to develop *claircognizance*, or clear-thought, using only your intuition to generate your answers from the crystal ball. I leave this for the last as it is not ideal for the beginner, carrying with it the burden of continuing to separate the analytical mind from the spiritual one, something that is difficult at best. However, if you continue to be unsuccessful with your other senses, you can pay attention to the gut feeling in the pit of your stomach or to emotional reactions that seem to come out of the blue when you hold your crystal in the trance state.

By this stage, I hope that at least one of the perceptions I've described has worked for you, but it is safe to proceed to the next step even if you have been unsuccessful with the perceptions. Sometimes, the process of asking questions of the crystal ball can seem to have the effect of increasing the output from the crystal ball dramatically, so there may have been subtle things that you did not notice before that will become amplified to the point of arresting your attention when you attempt a line of questioning.

Conversely, if more than one of the perceptions worked for you, I encourage you to try a calibration session separately for each of them. In order to calibrate, ask for your crystal ball to show you what a specific answer looks like, such as "show me yes" and "show me no," in order to feel more sure of the interpretations for what you are then shown. Ideally, you will eventually be able to use all your effective senses in concert when you are scrying, but training them individually in the beginning will make you a better reader by not allowing you to use the most comfortable one as a crutch as you learn.

If not all or if none of the perceptions is working for you, please do keep trying. As you keep practicing and studying, your discipline can help you attain other perceptions along the way, especially if you begin working with your dreams. You may find that meditation and dream interpretation can, over time, open the floodgates, allowing you easier access to your subconscious through other means. Don't be afraid to periodically push yourself to grow.

When acquiring any new skill, the ideal way to induce learning is to set a goal that is just above your current ability. Pushing yourself should ideally produce *cognitive dissonance*, an "aha moment" in which a whole new understanding becomes clear. However, in attempting to achieve this, you'll naturally have an equal if not greater number of "uh-oh" or "oh no" moments in which you are unable to make such a breakthrough. The only advice I can give is to seek out a mentor who is already deeply familiar with crystal ball reading and can be close to you, the student, to help advise you during your growth. But every individual is different, so even an apprenticeship can't be perfect. Whenever you set the bar a little too high, you can go back to your basic meditation and trance work, and try again later.

Example Readings

I am going to show you real examples of crystal ball readings in order for you to see how they might flow. In these examples, I am the reader and I refer to the client as "you."

A general reading on career and love

I see a ship capsizing, which may represent a failure in communication in a past relationship. You tend to give more than some others, so you have to be careful that you are not the one putting the most effort into a relationship. It can easily overwhelm both involved.

I see a man digging in the dirt with a shovel. This can represent a need to ground yourself in your life. That can mean more physical exercise and spending time with nature. This symbol can also represent needing to build a firm foundation for your career. You're good at what you do, but things may not be stable. As a result, perfectionism is less key than making sure you have all your bases covered.

I see smoke rising from a chimney in a home. You value stability very much, but you also need growth. It may be hard to get both. Stability should come first, of course. Then, instead of inciting imbalance with others, create change in yourself.

I see a man on a horse representing loyalty. Be careful that you are not loyal to a fault! This can represent events picking up very quickly with regard to love. It can also sometimes represent physical travel over land.

I see the capital letter *J*, if that means anything to you. It is near a hand that reaches for a musical note. This can represent a helpful person who wants to take care of you. Music associated with this person may mean that they have played a musical instrument, or it can also represent creativity and strong emotions.

General reading on career, love, and health

The first symbol I see is a wave hitting a bridge. You have the potential to get employment soon; however, you may temporarily have to do more work that your heart is not into. The good news is that you can work temporarily somewhere that can give you new connections and networking opportunities. For that reason, don't shy away from such jobs, as they may lead you to your dreams.

A strawberry indicates that by this summer you may be able to find an opportunity to make enough money to finance your creative goals.

I see an overturned cup by a broom. Though it is possible for you to marry your current partner, I would advise strongly against it. This suggests that resentment could grow between you, so I'm afraid that I do not see a good potential for growing love here. I would suggest ending the relationship yourself, if you choose to do so, as it does not look like he will end it.

I see a bottle floating in the water. Teaching and travel for you will begin with more learning. You are fed by knowledge and that can help you grow. Start small, and trust in your family and your friends as emotional support.

I see a pyramid balancing on a knife. Your intellectual and emotional health is greatly tied to your physical health. However, that doesn't mean that you are imagining issues. They are real, but they must be confronted in a balanced way as one won't go away without the other being managed.

Finally, I see a boline blade. There are things in your life that no longer serve you that need to be cut away to help you feel more free.

I hope that this reading makes sense and answers your questions for now. If you need clarification on any of these symbols, just ask!

Interpreting Symbols

For ease of reading, I will be writing this from the point of view of somebody who is interpreting visual symbols, but the concepts can be applied to other sensory perceptions as well. In fact, psychologists scoring the Rorschach inkblot test believe that other auxiliary observations during viewing of the inkblots are more important than the content— for example: the emotional reaction to what is seen, repeating content or similarities of color and form related to the content of what is seen, first impression of what is seen, or the thought process that goes into deciding what the shape represents based on its color and form.

Interpretation can be the most difficult part of divination. This is why, as a beginner, I'd like you to leave interpretation until after you've viewed all the symbols in your reading. Otherwise, you may be tempted to keep viewing symbols until you find one that you think is easier to interpret. Becoming comfortable with your intuition means that you need to trust your first perception, rather than second-guessing yourself.

It can be easy to attempt to cut corners. Just look at the many dream-interpretation dictionaries that litter the shelves of bookstores. Dream interpretation is a very valuable practice, but one person's dictionary may look nothing like another's. The authors of these books are well-meaning, and the suggestions may be helpful since we are all steeped in the same culture. However, to avoid many pitfalls, I would suggest laying them aside for beginners, and leave perusal of dream books for theoretical comparisons after you become comfortable with your own dream interpretations.

When building your own crystal ball dictionary, you likewise may be tempted to look up the meaning of the symbols. For interpretation, I believe that your inner resources should be your first references. Turn to external comparisons only after you have a solid hypothesis of your own. If you do add any understanding from the outside or from the inside, add it to your dictionary, noting the date. Your understanding will evolve over time.

For example, if I saw a bat in a crystal ball, it might mean something very different to me than to others. Personally, bats are my favorite animals. If I were to see a bat in a crystal ball for the first time, upon interpretation I would immediately assume that it was a good thing. The wings might suggest to me a message as well. If I turned to the interpretation dictionaries from a Western culture, I might find negative associations. For example, one symbol dictionary might say that a bat appearing means a death will happen in the family. This would not necessarily be true of my bat symbol, and I can tell you that it isn't. In

China, the bat signifies good luck; and in Navajo cultures, bats were messengers from dead loved ones. So, the bat, for me, might be a symbol of a good message from beyond.

In some cases, the relative arrangement in which the symbols appear are just as important as the symbols themselves. Upside-down symbols can represent the flip side of a situation. For example, a crown right-side up might represent regal and assertive behavior, while a crown upside down can represent bossy behavior. It doesn't always have to be negative. Aspects flipped upside down can show positive things as well. Also, pay attention to each symbol to see if it is made up of more than one symbol or object, as in three hearts instead of just one. Some symbols may be closely associated with one another. The clothes that a person is wearing, or all the things associated in a scene, can mean something quite different when alone. A whale in the water might mean to you something different from a beached whale. If symbols are shown far apart from one another, that has significance as well. For example, in a reading on potential compatible men, it may represent more than one potential if positive symbols are seen very far apart.

Letters and numbers can be a very special case. Their appearance as symbols in readings do make the crystal ball a tool that is much better than many others. However, they can also be riddles to be deciphered in each reading, especially if rushing your reading leaves you wondering in what order you saw them.

Pay attention to whether letters in your readings are upper or lower case. They may appear in order and complete to spell a word, or they may be jumbled out of order with some letters omitted, making yourself a word puzzle that can be solved with some patience and extra questioning. Take care not to guess, as that may be considered *cold reading*, which is the art of appearing to perceive more information from a person than you do. (I will discuss cold reading in more detail in chapter 6.) The temptation can be great, especially with first names, but I remind myself that there are many first names out there that I've never seen spelled or heard pronounced, so I wouldn't want to guess on one of those. If you have auditory perceptions during crystal ball reading, pay attention to those for pronunciation keys.

Capital letters in a row can often be initials in a name. Take special care not to make assumptions when you see letters that look the same uppercase as they do lowercase. Letters can also be associated with place names, adding another potential bit of confusion. Or such letters can even represent a prominent letter that can be seen at the place in question, such as a large letter on a billboard or building. Additional questions can help ahead of time. If you know you'll be looking for letters before you start, you may wish to ask some calibrating questions first about what it will look like if you see a place name as opposed to a person's name.

Numbers add a whole other piece of the puzzle. In addition to representing a date or an age, you also have the same location problem as with letters. The number may be part of a house or street number, for example, or it may be a prominent number shown on a sign or a parked car.

Ask first for the crystal ball to show you what the name of a place would look like, and then ask it to show you what the name of a person would look like. Hopefully there will be a clear difference between the two that can help you differentiate when such names come up.

You also have the added problem of the symbolic meaning of numbers, adding numerology to the mix. When you begin adding the symbolic meaning of numbers to your crystal ball dictionary, a good deal of meditation and analysis may need to go into your own personal understanding of numbers. For example, if you have synesthesia, you may associate colors or sounds with numbers. The Pythagorean system of numerology is different from the Chinese and others, so sometimes it is almost better the fewer associations you have to confuse you. Others may feel more comfortable with a full tool kit of interpretation! If you're already proficient with the tarot cards, be aware that you've been using numerology already, so pay attention to that part of you that has already been carefully trained.

One final aspect of numbers is that you can also count objects within the crystal ball. So even if you do not see the number three within the crystal ball, if you were, for example, to see three bells as one symbol within the crystal ball, you would interpret the symbol of the bell along with the symbolic meaning of the number three.

three

Grounding

I must admit that, when I first began my practice, I had some pretty idealistic and fantastic notions about what life as a professional fortuneteller would be like. I immediately signed myself up for every psychic fair and local festival within an hour's drive, and some quite a bit farther away. I imagined that all of us fellow crystal ball readers would band together like a romanticized version of a gypsy family, becoming fast friends and traveling together weaving our craft and spreading the good word about our art across the land.

At my first psychic fair, I set up hours early and then made the rounds—greeting everyone at every other table with a cheerful smile and a business card, only to be met with tired faces and people already grumbling about the exhausting day ahead. As the doors opened to the general public, I hurried back to my table in time to begin the day's rush. It was one stranger after another with a poker face, a mocking attitude, a sob story, or even pent-up frustration just looking for an outlet. But mixed in were also the high points of incredible discoveries and revelations that seemed to elevate the moments to intense emotional triumphs.

I was so distracted that I didn't even notice that the woman in the booth next to mine had packed up her things—until she was waving goodbye to let me know that she wouldn't be able to watch my booth during bathroom breaks. I took a brief moment between clients to ask her what was wrong, as it seemed to me she had been doing brisk business as well. She mumbled something about the day's business takings just not being worth her time and effort, and she beat a hasty retreat.

In the month following the fair, I tried to establish contact with my new friends from the fair, many of whom didn't seem to want anything to do with me due to competitive feelings or simply being much to busy with other jobs or obligations. When I returned to the fair a month later, armed with food to share with my new friends and conversation topics to pick up from last time, I was surprised to find more new faces than familiar ones. Later, clients I'd met at some of these fairs would ask me about other readers that had seemed to disappear from the face of the earth, asking me what happened to them since they were so good. I now believe that I know.

Just because a reader is very good at working with the crystal ball, and may naturally ground his or her own chi properly, doesn't mean that he or she is very good at grounding in a setting like a public fair, surrounded by many other people who have their own influences. Working all day at a psychic fair may amplify the back soreness from sitting, pain in the knees and feet from standing, as well as amplify the emotional wear and tear of working with so many people—and it can even lead to no longer seeing a spiritual purpose for psychic work. Yet these effects can all be mitigated and remedied with proper grounding techniques before, during, and after the event.

What Is Grounding?

Grounding is a process by which you are theoretically linked to the earth and to the present moment, even though your mind may be drifting to all sorts of places. A common grounding visualization is to imagine yourself as a tree, with a deep taproot pushing into the earth. It doesn't matter if you are several floors up or even on an airplane. Allow the imaginary connection to pass through any space and barriers to the earth. As you breathe in, imagine rejuvenating energy from the earth flowing up into your body and moving easily throughout it; and as you exhale, imagine that same life force flowing back into the earth.

If you skip this grounding method but find yourself getting headaches or feeling drained after scrying work, please go back and use this method or find a grounding method that works for you.

Grounding may seem unimportant to those who have lived their entire lives without doing it. Yet even if you are a skeptic, I encourage you to use grounding as a way to get yourself more quickly to a meditative state, allowing the routine of it to easily drop your brain waves from the heightened state of stressed alertness known as *beta waves* to the more sleepy state of *alpha waves*. I believe that the alpha waves are there to save you from growing tired too quickly and developing headaches, dizziness, or stomach-aches associated with exhaustion.

In my experience as a professional crystal ball reader, I've noticed that this is a very high turnover industry. I firmly believe that this is because psychic fairs are excellent places to expose poor grounding techniques. So many new people coming, one by one, and unloading their problems on the reader can easily create a state of stress, tiredness, and confusion. Grounding, in my experience, staves this off. In fact, I believe that knowing proper grounding techniques when I was a teacher (I was a middle-school and high-school science teacher for three years) served me very well for the same reasons. I imagine that other career people, such as waitresses and nurses, could benefit greatly from frequent and complete grounding.

A nineteenth-century French musician, François Delsarte, mapped out the emotional meaning behind parts of the body and gestures with a system that is still used by spiritual dancers today. Imagine your body made up of three sections: your head, your torso, and your lower body—with your lower body representing the physical, your torso representing the emotional, and your head representing the spiritual. Each of those main sections of the body can be broken down even further. For example, your feet represent the spiritual physical, which is why bare feet assist in grounding your connection with the earth for any work that involves the spiritual, to keep you feeling physically well with the easy flow of chi.

Pay attention to your perception of any feelings or imagery associated with any of these parts of your body. As an example, pain in your hips or lower abdomen may show that you are not fully grounded in the physical while you are reading the crystal ball. Warmth in your forearms may show that you are emotionally open and vulnerable during your reading. Your legs represent the emotional physical, and your hips represent the deeply physical. Your hands represent the emotional spiritual, which is why you should hold your crystal ball in your hands to connect your mind with your spirit during crystal ball gazing. Your forearms represent the purely emotional, and your shoulders represent the physical emotional. On your face, your mouth represents the physical spiritual, your cheeks represent the emotional spiritual, and your eyes and above represent the completely spiritual.

There is no such thing as too much grounding after divination or meditation. If you feel sick, it may be time for a day off from divination and meditation. If you repeatedly feel sick after a reading when you felt fine beforehand, that's a sign that you are not grounding yourself properly.

If you feel you are *too* grounded to be able to scry properly, you can wait to ground immediately afterward if you've mastered the practice, and you can even choose to fast to prevent the grounding process before scrying.

How I Learned Grounding

Grounding is not something that I learned early in childhood, though as a kid diagnosed with attention deficit hyperactivity disorder (ADHD), I have no doubt that the practice could have helped me during school and my daily tasks. Instead, things had to get worse in my life in order for me to discover the importance of grounding. When I was a teenager, some very strange and spooky things began to happen around me, as a young person who was very involved with magic and divination.

I may not have even noticed the early symptoms of not being properly grounded, such as moodiness, tension, and pains in my body, since that is easily a part of being a teenager. However, I did notice that some odd phenomena would happen in my room that seemed to be linked with my own heightened emotional state.

The first time this happened was when I awoke from a terrible dream, sat bolt upright in my bed, and watched a candle on my dresser appear to light itself. I got out of bed and extinguished it, assuming that the wick had simply been smoldering since I had lit the candle a few hours previously. My sleepy destruction didn't stop at candles. Once, as I slept in my college dorm room, my roommate watched me twitching comically from a bad dream, and then as I awoke, she witnessed the water glass by my bed explode in a shower of glass that fell in a circle everywhere but on my own body. She was fairly disturbed by this, and chose to move out.

I didn't realize that these seeming coincidences were actually a big problem until at one point I was in a very angry state, stormed into my room, slammed the door, and glared at my desk in time to watch a piece of paper seem to burst into flames along one edge. After putting out the tiny fire, I was terrified that I was developing some sort of paranormal problem that would end with me burning my parents' house down in my sleep. I decided that it was time to tell my mother about the strange happenings, and I was surprised to find that she had experienced odd phenomena during her teenage years as well. She suspected this time in a person's life is one of heightened and changing chi, which may not continue to regulate itself in the way it did previously.

Spiritual advisors of mine suggested that I begin to practice grounding, and after perfecting my own grounding with practice, I am happy to report that none of those uncontrolled incidents happened again. I also found that there were more mundane relaxation and concentration benefits that helped me with my studies in college as well as with my meditation and divination.

What You Need to Do in Order to Ground Yourself

Step 1: Settle yourself down and quiet your mind to observe yourself

Once you are experienced with grounding, you'll be able to do it automatically even on a crowded bus; but when you are first getting started, I suggest you treat each grounding as its own special meditation session. That means going to a quiet place where you won't be interrupted and turning off distracting telephones and lights.

Sit barefoot in a comfortable position and concentrate on your breathing, in order to attempt to clear your mind of the noise of everyday life and to focus on how you are feeling physically, emotionally, and spiritually. Notice where you feel tension or a sense of upset. You will be observing the change after you have finished grounding, so it is important to establish a baseline.

Step 2: Push out the negative chi and bring in the positive chi

This is most commonly done through visualization. Close your eyes and imagine any of that tension or upset as, for example, colored light. Imagine that light coursing down through your body to your feet and out the floor. You can continue to imagine it traveling out through the place in which you are located and into the earth. If you're in a tall building, it can go down the walls and through the foundation. If you are in a vehicle, it can be pressed out through the spinning tires into the earth. Even on an airplane it can fall like rain.

If you're not the sort who is good at imagining visual things, you can try using your other senses, such as your sense of touch, to slowly relax different muscle groups in your body from your head to your feet—first by tensing them, and then by releasing the tension. After you've done this, start a chi exchange with the earth by visualizing or feeling it coming back up into you so that you are balanced and not drained. For example, you might imagine beautiful colors creeping back up through the foundation of where you are seated and into your body, filling and energizing you.

Step 3: Check in with your body, mind, and spirit to make sure that you are grounded

Relax and analyze how you feel compared to when you began your grounding session. Is the tension or upset still there? It may be that you did not fully complete the phase where you pushed out the negative energy. Feel free to repeat. Do you feel sleepy or drained? It could be that you didn't pull enough fresh energy back up from the earth. Do you feel jittery, dizzy, moody, or cranky, or do you have a headache? It may be that you drew too much energy back up from the earth into you. Feel free to push out some of that positive energy until you feel that you've reached a place of equilibrium. This will take practice and experience until you feel personally comfortable.

If you feel unable to bring yourself to a comfortable place, there are some aids that can help you, such as holding a stone such as hematite in your hand, or eating a bit of food, or placing a bit of salt on your tongue. If you are unable to ground on your own, do use these crutches, but keep practicing to be able to do it without them. Conversely, if you have a hard time checking in with yourself beforehand, much less afterward, so you are unsure of whether grounding is actually doing anything at all, I encourage you to keep practicing and going through the motions. Over time, the acts of divination and meditation can increase your sensitivity to what is going on inside yourself. Ideally, after grounding you should feel relaxed, but also energized and ready to take on mentally strenuous tasks that involve concentration and a good attitude.

Step 4: Centering

As you grow more experienced, centering will probably start taking place during the first and third steps of grounding listed here, but as a beginner it is helpful to separate this step to make sure you're completely grounded after all three steps listed previously. *Centering* is the act of becoming present in the moment, in your own body at that time and place. It is vital not only for stepping out of mundane distractions before meditation or divination, but also for after practicing meditation or divination in order to return back to the real world.

To center, you can begin by checking in with your body, clearing your mind, and focusing on your breathing, as you did during the first and third steps in this sequence. But also, during centering, be aware of your environment and your place in the world and in the universe. Study the space around you and then close your eyes and attempt to re-create the space, the room you're in, through visualization, being mindful of where this location is on the planet and in all of creation.

Step 5: Shielding

Shielding is the practice of creating a boundary between your own personal chi and the chi of your environment, of others, and of external events that may be taking place. This step may be optional for some people, especially if you're alone in a familiar place or if you are purposely reading the energy of something or someone external to you. However, I encourage you to practice shielding when you are alone as a beginner, so that you can instantly engage this skill if you are feeling ungrounded due to an annoying emotional psychic vampire, a haunted house, a national tragedy, or anything else outside of yourself.

In order to shield, you should ground and center yourself, visualize a barrier between yourself and the external world, and practice holding a visualization until you find one that is easy to maintain and feels safe and secure to you.

It is best to shield only after grounding and centering, even if you feel that you need to defend yourself, because your own shield will alter the way that you ground and center. This is why it is important to frequently practice grounding and centering, so that you can do it quickly. Then, visualize a barrier between yourself and the external world. Those who can see auras often do this by strengthening the intensity or boundaries of the aura they already see. Some other common visualizations include a bubble, a circle of colored flames, or a rainbow of light that filters different things with each color.

Your shield will be highly personal and may depend on the situation, so experiment with different imagery and shield diameters. I know one person who visualizes a camping tent, another who imagines himself within a sarcophagus, and yet another who simply imagines transforming herself into a protective mother bear. Be aware that what works through one phase of your life may not work for another. I spent over a decade doing fine with a visualization of a ring of purple flames around myself, but when it suddenly stopped working, I was annoyed at how many people, especially odd strangers on the bus, would get in my personal space. I changed my visualization to one of guard dogs protecting me, and it worked like a charm. If you are having trouble with visualization, you can draw a circle around you with salt, chalk, flour, or a length of rope to help your brain see what it would look like if a boundary were traced around you.

Astral Travel and Ethereal Travel

Grounding is especially important for meditation or divination if you choose to attempt to cause your perceptions to leave your body. During *astral travel*—the process by which one's perceptions seem to be located on a supernatural or imaginary plane—some people experience the perception of a silver cord coming out of their body's belly button and attaching to the belly button of the astral person floating above. This is one way that you can visualize a link to the earth or to your body in order to find a way to ground or return.

There are myths circulating that if the cord is cut, the person traveling astrally will never be able to return to his or her body and instead will be a vegetable or a ghost. This is not true, and I can assure you that any cord perceived is quite indestructible. For those of you who are worriers, the biggest danger of astral travel is that you may not be able to respond to an emergency situation as quickly you might like, feeling overly groggy as you get back to the real world. Make sure, then, that you only travel astrally in safe and secure locations where you won't be disturbed. Turn off your phone and lock your doors. Those who practice forms of magic that occur within a magic circle should feel free to cast a circle, if doing so helps you feel more secure.

Ethereal travel refers to the out-of-body-experiences in which one is still perceiving the real world, but one's senses of perception seem to be coming to a source outside of one's body. This is a much more difficult phenomenon for some people to achieve, although others do it naturally, as I did. Those who wish to train for ethereal travel should begin by mastering meditation and astral travel, and should be able to control grounding so well that they can remain ungrounded for the period of ethereal travel and thoroughly ground afterward. Fasting for a day before ethereal travel may help the separation occur.

four

Symbols

A client contacted me, distraught because her two dogs, Sadie and Mollie, had run away from her home and she was desperate to know whether they were still alive and well—whether they would return home. If I were on location, I might have chosen to use pendulum dowsing to track the dogs down on the spot. However, this reading was performed over a distance, and the client could not provide a map to me of the area in which her dogs were located for a proper pendulum dowsing.

I elected instead to use the crystal ball to show me as much information as possible. Gazing into the crystal ball, I saw one of the dogs immediately, and I described a mutt who seemed to have some Labrador in her. The client confirmed that this was Mollie, just as I saw Mollie and the other dog running up a driveway that curved to the left with a blue truck and a dilapidated steel shed. The client told me that this described her truck and driveway, so I was happy to say that they looked alive enough that they would return home.

Eager to find them, she asked me where they were at the moment. I began to spell out some letters and numbers that began coming to me from the crystal ball, but they were jumbled. There was an *S* and then the number *4*, and as I named some more letters, my client was able to unscramble them to a street name. She took her truck down the road to the street in question and found a house number that had those numbers, hearing her dogs barking from that house's backyard! She was so thankful that she was able to bring them home.

How I Learned to Interpret Symbols

Though seeing the shapes came naturally and easily to me, puzzling out the more cryptic and symbolic messages from the crystal ball was a longer process for me to learn, and is ongoing for me. It began as simple mental associations. When I was a child, many of my senses seemed to be naturally linked. Whenever I thought of the number *4*, my visual field would see the color green quite strongly. In the same way, certain sights would be linked with smells. Music, especially, would be associated with lights and colors that affected even my sense of touch. When attending the symphony, whenever I heard the loud clash of the symbols, I also saw a bright flash of white light. The same flash of light would appear when I heard the percussive sound of hands clapping.

Once, when I had injured myself and was in pain, I saw the usual ribbons of light when listening to music and I allowed myself to visualize them wrapping around my leg, the area of my body that was currently experiencing pain. As long as I held this image, I was able to ward off the physical sensation of pain from my own body. Later, I learned that the ability to blend senses together in this way is called *synesthesia*. My mother experienced this as well, and shared her experiences with me, so I did not realize that associating colors with numbers and all the other sense blending was not a normal part of life until I was nearing adulthood.

As a young adult in college, I became fascinated with the Jungian psychology of symbols and the repeating archetypes of the Hero's Journey found in literature. During my personal spiritual study, I loved to learn about deities that had crossed all borders, such as the Celtic goddess Brigid, who is also found as a Catholic saint and even as a Vodou *loa*, among other things. I was amazed at common symbols that would pop up across cultures around the globe, even those separated geographically and through time, so that they weren't just picking up cues from each other. I began to experience that there are specific symbols, archetypes, and stories that arise from the common human experience, or even the collective unconscious of everyone who is alive today or who has ever lived. It became part of my life's purpose as a crystal ball reader to not only understand the symbols of others, but also to process the deep unconscious symbology of my own mind.

As I continue on my learning path, I find myself vacillating between looking outside myself and looking within for meaning, and I believe that to be a natural part of my growth as a reader. As a beginner, I hungrily devoured books on symbols, especially any that had a huge dictionary full of nouns that each had deeper meaning, such as dream interpretation books. Every once in a while, after reading something that completely did not mesh with my own internal understanding, I would swear off other people's symbols for a while and focus on generating my own meanings. But soon I'd be back to the books, or pumping other people or cultures for information, ever searching for the individual or group of people who were somehow the authority on the matter. As a beginner, I encourage you to explore both the external and the internal.

List of Symbols and What They Mean to Me

Example Number	Meanings
1	Being alone or an individual. Birth, aggressiveness, certainty, new beginnings, breakthrough, potential.
2	Balance and harmony. Union between two people, ease, necessary choice, priority

change, juggling responsibilities, new door-
way, tension.

3 Creation after the union of two. Communication. Growth, life, heartbreak, perfecting,
journey, meeting with old friends.

4 Stability, home, saving money, keeping
secrets, feeling trapped, patience required,
meeting a new friend. In Chinese interpretation, 4 can be unlucky, representing suffering
and death.

5 Activity, instability, financial loss, disappointment, a game, death, breakup destruction, give and take.

6 Change and progression, study, journey and
leadership, transition, communication, celebration, generosity.

7 Mystery, consciousness, trickery, spirituality,
cutting and pruning, a new perspective.

8 Steady gain of power through work, pros-
perity, getting the word out, safety, seeking
deeper meaning and moving on.

9 Change, good luck, nearing completion and
rebirth, barriers to be overcome, success, stress.

Example Symbolic Interpretations

Airplane: A plane can obviously indicate travel by air. If it is
facing to the right, it can indicate travel to a new place

that someone has never been before. Facing to the left means that it is a return to a place of the past. If the plane is heading up or crashing down, it can represent escapism.

Alligator: This symbol represents a hidden asset, possibly a quite dangerous one! Take care to notice the alligator's position with respect to the symbol of water, as that may add to the meaning of its appearance. For example, an alligator mostly in the water may represent somebody holding in emotions until they become a problem. Half in and half out of water, the alligator represents the versatility needed to hide that dark side when needed, but also bring it out into the light. If the alligator is entirely on land, this can represent the calm before the storm!

Anchor: A lack of progress that is under the control of a person. When seen in a relationship reading, it can be positive if the person is seeking stability or negative if the person is seeking progress.

Apple: An apple represents the fruit of knowledge. Seeing an apple in the crystal may indicate the need to undergo a course of study, or the need to teach. An apple can also be a health sign, as in "An apple a day keeps the doctor away!"

Arrow: Pay attention to where the arrow is pointing. An arrow pointing to the left can ask the person to look to his or her past, childhood, or roots, while an arrow pointing to the right can represent looking to the future and travel. An arrow pointing up can represent growth, while an arrow pointing down represents a need to break things down to achieve stability.

Axe: Like the scythe, the axe symbol means that something may need to be cut short. However, it may show that something short-lived can still be helpful and productive.

Baby carriage: This can show that a baby is on the way!

Bat: Good news from somebody who is dead. Messages from the beyond!

Bear: The bear is a protective symbol, but it can represent the kind of protection that is unpredictable or not to be relied upon.

Bell: A call to action that may not be ignored. This can also represent marriage bells.

Bird: Communication with somebody from a distance. The bird can also represent traveling somewhere by air. A bird facing to the left means somebody or someplace from the past, while a bird facing to the right means someone or someplace new. A perched bird represents the need to keep a watchful eye on things before progressing, and perhaps needing to move a different way than originally planned. A flock of birds traveling to the right can mean good luck, while a flock traveling to the left can be a bad sign, unless the birds are owls, in which this is reversed. Owls traveling to the left is a good sign, and to the right is negative. Eagles, hawks, or other birds of prey can represent vigilance and can also represent nationalism. Owls represent wisdom as well as nighttime. Doves symbolize peace. Pay attention to seasonal birds that may hint at a time frame.

Boat: Emotional communications. The appearance of a boat may suggest a need to balance giving and receiving emotional feelings in the form of words with someone. The boat can also represent travel over water. If the boat is facing to the left, this can be associated with people from the past, while facing to the right means someplace or someone new. A ship capsizing represents a failure to communicate.

Book: A course of study that should be undertaken, and can also represent either a figurative or literal journey. A book can also represent the occult. A book held by a person shows his or her love of ideas and intelligence.

Bottle: This can have several meanings. A bottle of alcohol can indicate substance abuse or over-celebration. A message in a bottle may mean communication that is taking too long coming out. At other times, bottles can represent emotional travel.

Bridge: This indicates an opportunity that, once taken, has a point of no return. Take a look at the state of the bridge seen to decide whether it is a good opportunity that should be taken. Is the bridge flooded, without a foundation, or falling apart? Is it on fire, meaning that it is being transformed? In that case, it isn't a good idea to cross, especially if you want to come back! Is the bridge secure and pleasing to the eye? Then it may be time to make a move!

Broom: Marriage, representing jumping over the broom during the marriage ceremony. A falling broom can represent visitors coming soon. A sweeping broom can represent the need to clear out old negativity.

Bull: Taurus, stubbornness, rage.

Butterfly: A symbol of positive transformation. This is not the gentle kind of change that slow growth creates, but a radical shift that can be disruptive but greatly needed.

Candle: A lit candle is included with the symbol of fire to represent dynamic energy. It can represent an idea that can provide the spark to get started, or an old flame.

Car: Describe the car, if reading for another person, because sometimes this can represent a real person's actual car. A car is also a symbol of travel, and when pointed left represents travel to a place known from the past; when pointing right, it represents travel to a new place. A car can tell a lot about a person. A race car, for example, may indicate a thrill-seeker!

Carrot: Carrots, or other root plants, can show a need for somebody to be more grounded, stable, or to look locally for what they seek.

Cat: A feline is a feminine symbol and can represent magic and witchcraft. Often cats are seen as witches' familiars, creatures that aid magical work.

Chair: A need to wait, often a message of stability. When in a career reading, a chair can represent the potential to take a new position that offers more stability.

Chameleon: Protection through trickery. Needing to become one with the situation and go with the flow to avoid stress or danger.

Circle: A repeating cycle that has happened several times and will happen again. The circle can also represent protection, and what a person values, especially if it surrounds another symbol.

Cloak: A cloak on a person represents somebody who must hide away for a time in order to discover what they truly want and need while being protected from those who would judge.

Clothes: Clothes seen off of a person—for example, a shirt lying on the floor—represent an inability to fit into a role in life. The nature of the clothes—including their color, age, gender association, or whether they are part of a uniform—may give more clues about the role. Torn clothes may mean that time in life in which a role was fulfilled has been destroyed in such a manner that a person cannot return to that former life.

Clown: False emotion and immaturity.

Club: A club of any shape can represent the same things as the wand symbol, as the suit in the regular playing card deck corresponds to that suit in the tarot deck. That is, it can represent the fiery energy of sexual chemistry, new life, or creativity.

Coin: Coins can represent material wealth. Coins can also represent physical health and property.

Comb: A comb can represent getting caught up in unimportant or shallow details that distract from the true priority of the situation. This symbol can suggest applying that same careful scrutiny to your true focus.

Cornucopia: This is the horn of plenty and represents abundance, especially of fertility or wealth.

Crab: This is the symbol of the zodiac sign for Cancer. It is feminine, and represents emotional feelings and desire for family and comfort.

Cross: A cross can represent a Christian faith connection, protection, or change that is about to occur as the result of somebody being at a crossroads in life.

Crown: A need to get attention and to seize leadership, a crown indicates a person who, at least, should *think* that he or she is in charge!

Cup: Representing water, emotions, and the west. An upright cup can be a positive symbol representing a potential for love, while an overturned cup can represent an emotional loss.

Deer: A male deer can indicate the maturity of a person involved with or in the reading, depending on how the antlers appear.

Devil: A devil or demon represents one's own negativity. This can show that the person in the reading is his or her own worst enemy. It also represents procrastination and encourages action in order to get past this delay.

Diamond: The diamond is a symbol of earth and can represent wealth, friendship, the physical, and the material. In the regular playing card deck, it corresponds to the pentacles symbol in the tarot deck.

Dinosaur: A dinosaur is a symbol of the distant past. This may be a message for somebody to investigate the past, even if it is the sort of past that nobody is around or willing to talk about anymore.

Dog: A symbol of deep loyalty, to family and friends especially. The dog can represent loyalty to a fault, in cases where a person is used.

Doorknob: This is the sign of a new potential that could change the world of a person. However, it must be initiated by the person who wants it to happen, as it won't all happen on its own!

Dress: The role of a woman, especially a married woman. Like a uniform for men, the dress for women can show a specific profession or station in life.

Egg: Fertility and creation. The egg represents a project that may be long overdue to bring into manifestation.

Elephant: The elephant represents memory, especially memory of ancestors or elders. The elephant also represents a message that can't be ignored.

Eye: The eye is traditionally a protective symbol. In some cultures people adorn themselves with a representation of the "evil eye" to ward off witchcraft or bad intent. The eye asks you to be very wary and alert to danger, especially from a person who does not bear you good intentions! An eye can also represent awareness of the spiritual.

Fan: A hand fan or electric fan can represent a need to help out the winds of change! Just as you can fan the flames of a fire, the fan can show that extra bit of your own initiative that is needed before you can fully transition from one situation to another.

Feather: A bird's feather is a symbol of air, so a feather can represent the intellect and intuition. It can also ask somebody who is very intelligent to "lighten up" a little bit and not overthink the situation.

Fire: In addition to being associated with passion and the direction of the south, a fire associated with any other symbol represents transformation. This transformation may be a good thing, but it is not gradual and the change may seem devastating to those who value stability. The feather can also represent justice, as the ancient Egyptians believed that a person's heart would be weighed on a scale opposite a feather after death.

Fish: Sometimes seen as the salmon of wisdom, the fish traditionally symbolizes knowledge or study. Pay attention to the direction the fish is traveling. If the fish is facing to the left, this study may have to do with a childhood pursuit or ancestry, while if pointing to the right will aid the future. A leaping fish represents learning a skill that can be directly applied. A fish is surrounded by water, so this symbol associates the study and learning with something that is very emotional or creative to the person.

Flag: Nationality, needing to get in touch with ethnic roots. This can also represent travel to or work in another nation.

Flower: While a flower in itself can represent new love beginnings, fertility, and femininity, pay attention to whether you can tell what type of flower it is, as this is often a symbol of the season. For example, in a love reading a blooming tulip or daffodil can represent a new relationship forming in the spring. A water lily can represent the summertime. Red roses mean passionate love, while yellow roses mean friendship. White roses can honor a respectable occasion of bonding. A blossom that has just opened shows something new and fragile.

Food: Images of various types of food may indicate a need for grounding. Food can also offer clues about seasons. If a food is very closely associated with a tradition for a certain time of year, this may indicate a timeline associated with the reading. For example, a turkey might point your attention toward the Thanksgiving holiday. When I saw a turkey in a reading for a client, she told me that Thanksgiving that year fell on her wedding anniversary, and the context of the reading turned to unresolved issues with her ex-husband.

Foot: A bare foot represents sensitivity, a need for grounding, being in touch with nature, and the spiritual. In some religious traditions, the bare foot represents purity and cleanliness. Feet represent the spiritual aspect of what is material and physical.

Forearm: A prominent position of the forearm in the human form or a perception within your own forearms represent emotional vulnerability, usually deliberate.

Goat: A goat can represent resilience, versatility, and when in a reading on relationships, can show the stubborn way in which two people push each other's buttons!

Graduation cap: Since a hat represents leadership, a graduation cap represents this attribute with regard to schooling. Sometimes this can also indicate a quite literal graduation for those in college, and can be used for timing other activities recommended by other symbols.

Gun: A gun represents focused energy. Note whether it is pointed right, indicating the future, or left, indicating the past. For example, a gun pointing to the left can show a need to eliminate negativity from the past. A gun firing represents decisive action that has already been put into play, while a gun being checked by a hand can ask you to be prepared with any "ammunition" you may need before you proceed. A hunting gun can show that hunting is the hobby of a person.

Hand: The interpretation of a hand depends on what the hand is doing. If the hand is pointing, look to the interpretation of an arrow. If the hand is open with the palm upturned, this may indicate the need to receive help. If the hand is palm downward, this may indicate the need to take or to be more generous. A gloved hand shows a job that needs to be done. A palm facing the reader means a need to stop and protect oneself, especially from giving too much effort or money. Hands represent the spiritual aspect of the physical and the material.

Hat: Represents taking on a leadership role, or taking on a new role.

Head: The human head represents the seat of all things spiritual. Pay attention to the expressions that the face holds for emotional messages. Clear features may indicate a real person, so take note of hair, skin, and eye color as well as any other identifiable features if relaying this information to someone else. A head facing to the left refers to people in the past, and to the right represents people in the future.

Heart: Love and emotion, showing where one's passion lies. Interpersonal interactions. The heart can represent somebody's emotional health and well-being. A cracked heart can represent miscommunication that leads to heartbreak. In a deck of regular playing cards, the suit of hearts corresponds to the suit of cups in a tarot deck.

Hips: Hips or the rear end of a human form represent the physical, especially sexuality. Movement of the hips represents power rooted in the earth and material things.

Horn: This can have many meanings. It can represent the "horn of plenty," showing abundance. It can also be a literal musical instrument that somebody used to play or still plays. The horn can also represent advice. When pointing to the left, it is from somebody in the past. When pointing to the right, it is from somebody in the future.

Horse: Can be a symbol of loyalty. The horse can also represent travel over land. If the horse is facing left, it may be to a place that has been visited before, especially the home of an old friend or family. Facing to the right means travel to a place that has not yet been visited.

Horseshoe: Traditionally a symbol of good luck; when the curve points downward, it can represent an opportunity one may have been waiting or saving up for. When the curve points upward, it can represent losing a good chance or, if it is above another symbol, it can represent that symbol in a very fortunate light.

House: A symbol of stability, the house can represent the ability to secure a good living space for family. A house that looks as if it may fall over or is upside down, however, can show instability, or the feeling of being trapped by home and family. Smoke rising from the chimney of a home is from the hearth fire and represents a need for growth, perhaps meaning a move or the birth of children.

Key: This represents one action that must be taken before progression can occur. This symbol can also represent privacy or the need to keep secrets.

Keyhole: A keyhole means that somebody is being too picky looking for the right fit! The keyhole can be seen on another symbol, such as a heart showing a person who has high standards for a lover; or a coin, showing somebody being too choosy with job opportunities.

Knife: Like the sword, this represents the intellect, but like the axe it can also represent a need to cut away things that are no longer serving a person. This must be done by his or her own hand.

Lantern: Associated with the symbol of fire, a lantern held by a person represents a creative light that he or she must let shine. It is contained right now, but for too long, and the person is seeking a way to properly express the self.

Leaf: This represents impermanence and the fragility of even the very strong. It can also represent a source of energy and strength during such times. A falling leaf can indicate autumn or, more metaphorically, can show that some old things have reached the end of their cycle and must be shed for a better cycle to begin. If you can identify the leaf, it may also indicate a location.

Legs: Prominent legs in a human form represent the emotional connection to the physical and material things. They can also represent either a literal or metaphorical journey when depicted in motion, or a period of waiting when shown in a seated position.

Lightning: This can represent extreme change in a person's life. This is the kind of change that, while not pleasant, is necessary. Lightning seen in one's crystal ball prompts advice to find friends and family for emotional and financial support.

Lion: A lion represents authority that can be dangerous. The lion can often show up when there is a boss who is preventing a promotion, or a similar strong opposition.

Lobster: The lobster is associated with the moon, and thus femininity, cycles, and fear. The lobster is also associated with the waters of emotion.

Mask: A mask is a protective symbol against emotional or physical attack. If the eyes are emphasized, it can show that the person concerned is more vulnerable than he or she lets on.

Monster: Monsters seen in the crystal ball are often personifications of inner struggles or parts of a persona. Other aspects of the monster may need to be carefully analyzed before you can name the emotion or personality trait that it represents, including the color of the monster and aspects that represent its demeanor. If the monster is a gargoyle, it is a positive protective symbol even if it does look angry!

Moon: Generally a symbol of femininity and fertility, a full moon can also represent fear and repeating cycles that happen emotionally in one's life. A waxing moon, curving with the points pointing to the right, represents growth, especially creative potential. A waning moon, with the points to the left, indicates a need to clear space in one's life emotionally to make room for new, creative projects. The moon also represents spirituality and a need to pay attention to dreams for messages.

Moth: The moth represents subtlety, mystery, and fear of the unknown.

Mouse: A mouse asks you to pay very close attention to the details! If you're a big-picture person, sometimes you may be overlooking something small that is the real point!

Mountain: A mountain represents the higher self. So, if somebody is climbing a mountain, it can show that he or she is seeking deeper meaning in love or trying to improve in a career path. Look at other symbols that may be on the mountain, such as trees representing family and ancestry or other animals. A mountaineering pickaxe may indicate that somebody is undertaking desperate measures for self-improvement that may not turn out well.

Mouth: A mouth represents a message to be communicated that has to do with the physical world. Sometimes it can represent a warning of imminent danger that can be avoided. The expression of the mouth can alter this meaning to particular emotions. For example, expressions of rage, disgust, surprise, or loving kisses can be shown representing themselves.

Mushroom: This can indicate the person being read is so helpful that he or she takes on many burdens of others. The mushroom shows that others may be unsupportive or may feed off of and use the person's energy for their own means. Those needy others may need to be cut off or helped to become more independent before too much draining is done or before dependence is developed.

Musical instrument: Many musical instruments turn out to be associated with an actual person. For example, seeing a guitar in a reading to find the characteristics of a suitable potential husband may tell you that he played the guitar in the past or still plays it. A horn, however, can represent a call to action that can't be ignored. The horn can appear as any type, such as a trombone or a trumpet. Other examples of musical instruments that I've seen in the crystal ball include the flute and the violin.

Musical note: This can be a symbol showing a love of music and playing an instrument, or a person to get the emotional word out in creative means. When psychic John

Edward sees a musical note when performing a reading, he believes that it means prayer.

Pen: This is a strong sign that writing is in order, especially a book! The pen is also, ironically, associated with the sword. So, in the case of crystal ball reading at least, the pen is not quite mightier than the sword, but is its equal.

Person: Though the posture of a person can often be symbolic, most people I see in my crystal ball turn out to represent very real people. Whenever you spot a person, take careful note of descriptive features to share if reading for another. Communicate the gender, build, hair length and color, clothing, position, direction the person is facing, expression, and approximate age if you can. The position of the person can be more symbolic. For example, a person climbing a mountain can be shown as trying to seek lofty heights. People back to back cannot face each other until at least one compromises.

Pyramid: This represents emotional and spiritual stability.

Rabbit: Symbol of fertility and abundance. This can represent physical fertility, which should be communicated if reading for another person, even if it alarms him or her, and can also represent having an abundance of money.

Rings: Rings can represent marriage. They also represent eternity and cycles. When two rings are interlocked, it means that cycles from the past must be linked to those from the future.

Rock: A rock can be a sign of how stable the situation is. Notice whether the rock is sitting firmly on the ground, indicating safety, or whether the rock is teetering on an edge or cracked, indicating a precarious situation.

Rocket: This shows ambitions that need to take flight, otherwise there can be destruction! A rocket can also be a masculine symbol.

Rolling pin: This represents efforts that one person makes to try to make another person conform. Most often seen in relationship and family readings, this effort is usually one-sided and is resented on both sides.

Rope: A cord or rope can bind symbols together so that they cannot be separated. A person who is bound with rope can be symbolically held prisoner by another person, either spiritually or emotionally.

Scythe: A symbol of death, this is a clear sign that something needs to be cut off. This can mean quitting a job or breaking up a relationship. Note if there is anything near the scythe that it could be said to be cutting. This symbol can also be represented by a boline blade, which is a half-moon-shaped hand knife.

Seashell: Needing to use creativity in order to express emotions in a positive way to avoid destruction or a feeling of being overwhelmed.

Seed: A seed represents creativity and the potential for a huge project to be undertaken. If the seed is recognizable, it may also show a seasonal clue indicating the time frame.

Seedlings: The growth of seedlings in a crystal ball are often seen in numbers, which can have meaning. Ostensibly, a group of seedlings is a good sign, showing many potentials. However, the red flag here is that, if one waits, they can grow to be a barrier to progress. Also, in numbers, they can distract and be difficult to choose between, causing the person to not be able to see the forest for the trees!

Shepherd's crook: A means of giving gentle guidance to somebody who needs a light touch.

Shield: In addition to being a protective symbol, this also indicates that you must do battle rather than run away from something. If a shield is also seen with a sword, it means you must fulfill this role and fight this fight, otherwise you or somebody you love may be hurt or the same battle may crop up again later in another form.

Shoe: A shoe, depending on its type, can represent somebody's business role, such as a high-heeled shoe for a woman. A shoe can also represent needing to pound the pavement to search for a job, needing to do some detective work to find out the truth about a situation, or it can represent travel over land. A shoe pointing to the right is travel to a new place, while a shoe pointing to the left can represent going to a place of the past. A boot can represent work and responsibility.

Shoulders: Shoulders represent emotional passion and sensuality. Shaking shoulders can represent trying to get sexual attention or enjoyment of something that appeals to emotional pleasure.

Signpost: This can tell somebody to sit up and take notice, but it may be of passing relevance, such as a sign on the side of the road during a long journey.

Skeleton: A symbol of death, the skeleton represents negativity that may have been tolerated or hidden but that must be eliminated in order to make room in life for more positive things. Relationship readings that show skeletons may indicate that baggage from past relationships affects a current relationship.

Snake: This symbol can vary in its interpretation due to the fear that some have of serpents. Traditionally, the snake represents long life and health. This may indicate that healing or the cycle of life and death should be a focus for the reading.

Snowflake: This can represent creativity and originality of an emotional nature. Snow and ice can represent the cold and cruel emotions of another. Snow can also quite literally refer to wintertime.

Spade: In a deck of playing cards, the suit of spades corresponds to the suit of swords in a tarot deck. Thus, these two symbols are equivalent, representing the intellect as well as aloofness. If the spade is shown in the act of digging, it can represent using one's mind to dig deeper into an issue that may be specified by another symbol being unearthed. If the spade looks more like a shovel, it is a more earthy symbol, indicating the need for grounding and building a strong foundation. If you see a trowel planting seeds, this may show a need for those things to happen before a new beginning can occur.

Spider: This symbol's meaning can vary, as some people do have a fear of spiders. However, the traditional meaning of the spider is that of creation, as the spider is the weaver of a web. The web can represent community, deceit, tradition, or protection.

Square: The appearance of squares represents how important stability is to the person concerned. Squares can represent a need to be very conservative financially or to save money. A square can also represent needing to keep a secret, or to play your cards close to your chest with some people!

Star: A star can represent pure hopes and dreams that must be pursued, even when some of the original goals may have been unrealistic. A five-pointed star or pentagram is a symbol of the earth and material things such as money.

Strawberry: This can represent the summer season, sensuality, and a sweet reward.

Sun: This symbol cautions against burnout through over-focus, but is in general a positive symbol. The sun represents growth in all areas of life in harmony.

Sword: Conflict and communications gone wrong. Intellect and writing. Communications over a distance, in these modern times suggesting over the telephone or the Internet. A sword pointing to the left may represent a need to contact somebody from the past, while a sword pointing to the right may suggest contacting somebody new.

Table: A table represents stability, the home, and a secure and safe location.

Texture: Seeing a lot of surface texture on something within the crystal ball—for example, spiky or smooth objects and raised patterns—represents a desire for closeness in a relationship, as it also does in the scoring of the Rorschach inkblot test.

Thimble: A sign of protection during detail work. A thimble seen in the crystal indicates that somebody needs to take care of himself or herself with some minor lifestyle changes or precautions that could save the day.

Torso: A human chest is the place of the heart, and represents the root of all emotional expression. Female breasts can also represent nurturing motherhood and fertility.

Tower: A tower represents imprisonment or a feeling of being trapped. In some readings, a tower can represent jail time. If the tower is tilted, it represents a poor foundation. It can often be an indicator that a relationship will not last.

Tree: A tree and its network of branches immediately may refer to a family tree. The tree asks a person to become more stable, perhaps needing to reach out to family for emotional or financial support. A tree can also represent ancestral roots and seeking stability through finding that deeper connection to such roots. The type of tree, if identifiable, can indicate a location (for example, a palm tree can indicate travel to the tropics), while the appearance of the tree can indicate a season to help you find the timeline of events. Seasonal effects on trees can also be symbolic, as a tree without leaves may show that there are no resources to give at this time.

Triangle: Make sure that you check the definition for an "arrow" if the triangle appears to be an arrow. The triangle is associated with the number three, and represents the instability that is necessary in order for growth to occur. A triangle can represent getting together with old friends in order to work toward a common goal.

Turkey: Can represent the American and Canadian Thanksgiving holidays as the traditional food. Thus, it can represent the giving of thanks that is the sentiment for the season. A turkey can also be a derogatory symbol indicating a clueless and clumsy person.

Uniform: A person wearing a uniform can represent a career role, especially in the case of the military representing military affiliation.

Wall: A barrier that must be considered before progress can be made.

Wand: A staff or a line that looks like a wand represents fire and the direction of the south. It represents a need to strike out on a path and take action. This can represent passion and sexual chemistry.

Water: Water represents emotions, so any body of water in the crystal ball or in a dream can represent a potential for overwhelming emotions. Water can also represent intuition and a dreamlike state that can often be fooled or tricked by an illusion.

Well: A well indicates a deep emotional reserve at hand. It may suggest a need to reserve your feelings for something important, or to keep secret those feelings that need protection.

Wing: A single wing of a bird, angel, or bat represents one person working harder than another person in a relationship. This unequal strength can make sure that there is no progression (think of one oar in the water of a rowboat). This can build resentment. Two wings can give extra energy and impetus to whatever symbol it is attached.

Wolf: Spirituality and sacredness, protection, practicality, strength.

How to Determine What Symbols Mean to You

In your trance state, the first request you might ask for is, "Show me what *yes* is like." Allow the crystal plenty of time to respond to your question, but write down the first thing that you perceive. Ask it to show you what *no* is like, and do the same. You should now have enough preparation to perform a simple reading that gives you a positive or negative answer.

You can return to this calibration state whenever you like. In fact, it is a useful practice when visual readers spy a symbol in the crystal but just can't wrap their heads around what it means in response to a question. That will be a natural occurrence for all perceptions when you're still learning the language of your crystal ball, and you'll be forced to have a meditation session where you puzzle over what that symbol or other perception means to you. Note that I did not give you the option of asking the question over and over again until you get a clear answer. Even though it will be frustrating at first, you must learn the nature of your own personal symbols or perceptions. However, you can circumvent such frustration by phrasing your question as a *yes* or a *no*, or by asking a calibrating question before you ask the main question.

For example, if you are trying to decide between a medical-school focus of radiology or internal medicine, you might simply ask the crystal, "Should I focus on radiology or internal medicine?" An experienced reader, fluent in the language of symbols, may be able to interpret anything that came from the crystal. But a new reader, and even an experienced reader who wants things to be absolutely clear, might rephrase the question or calibrate the crystal for the question by breaking it into two questions. "Should I focus on internal medicine?" would be the first question. Such a reader would then wait for a yes or no answer before making sure by asking, "Should I focus on radiology?" Or, as a reader you could ask, "Show me internal medicine" and wait for the answer. Then ask, "Show me radiology" before asking the final question as it was originally phrased: "Should I focus on radiology or internal medicine?"

At this point, your *yes* and *no* should be written down in your notebook to flesh out your own personal crystal ball dictionary. Writing your dictionary should begin right away since you have a whole inner language to learn. I suggest keeping it in a three-ring binder, or any other way that you can move pages around as you add to it, and not just for alphabetizing. Your interpretations of your perceptions may change with time and experience, so you want to be able to document how they've changed. Ideally, you'll have a page for each word, as well as a journal with notes on entire readings to document future predictions that come to pass. Make sure you write the date by anything that you add to your dictionary. You'll be surprised how your understanding can evolve.

If you are a visual perceiver, the interpretations of the symbols in the crystal ball are very likely to match the interpretation of what you see in your dreams. For that reason, working with your dreams may be a very important exercise that can speed up your ability to read with your crystal ball.

Indeed, keeping a dream journal is the first advice I give to people who wish to develop their own psychic abilities.

Even though you can add your dream symbols to your crystal ball dictionary, you should also keep a separate dream notebook so that you can write out your dreams with as much detail as you can. It is important to keep this journal within reach of your bed since as soon as you awake, your brain waves resume their usual waking format, essentially losing the trance state of sleep and causing you to forget your dreams. If you can never remember your dreams anyway, consider taking a vitamin B-complex supplement. If your inability to remember dreams is accompanied by an inability to achieve restful sleep, it may be time for a trip to the doctor.

The next part is the hardest part of all. It takes a lot of willpower to write in a dream journal rather than rolling over and going back to sleep. Write in your dream journal before a trip to the bathroom in the night. Consider keeping a small flashlight with your pen and notebook so that you won't wake up your significant other. Even set the alarm a few extra minutes early on your alarm clock to give you time to record your dreams. This could be an essential part of your spirituality if you allow your dream vision to take flight. Face this challenge with discipline, as you would any other serious study.

When you've recorded your dreams, come back to them once a month and highlight any events that were *precognitive*, meaning that they foretold an event that later came to pass. Read through your dreams and circle all the words that are also symbols. On another page, you can tally how many times symbols reoccur in your dreams. These are ones to analyze and to take to meditation.

Using meditation for interpretation is suggested to allow more free associations to flow. Interpreting some symbols will be easy for you without meditation, if you have a strong reaction to them, as I would with a bat. If you have synesthesia, and your senses blend together, associations will come easily as well, since each symbol may have a color, a feel, or a taste. But some symbols will be downright puzzling. If you take your crystal to meditate, once you enter the trance, you can push out all thoughts from your mind except only that symbol. Pay attention to any emotions or perceptions that may arise during meditation as well.

Frustratingly enough, the meaning of some symbols will only become clear with experience. For example, there is one specific tarot card with only one specific deck that I own that seemed to decide for itself that it wanted to mean an automobile accident. When a friend first gave me the deck as a teenager, I eagerly went about learning to interpret with it. Since each deck artist's interpretations may differ, I used the book to help me. The book for this specific deck gave the interpretation of the Two of Swords to mean "a parting of ways."

So, whenever I got to that card in the past, I would tell the client that he or she had just parted ways with something once known. Whenever I saw it in the future, I would say that the client was about to part ways with something. The first person who got the Two of Swords in a reading with my new deck furrowed her brow when I read her past interpretation. "I don't know if this is a 'parting of ways,'" she said, "but I just totaled my car!" We thought a bit and decided it could be a match, but it was a stretch. When I read for a gentleman who got the Two of Swords in his past as well, he waited until after the reading to give me feedback. He told me that everything had been right on except the past interpretation. He had just recovered from a serious auto wreck and was hoping that the reading would touch on that.

Over time, as this pattern kept repeating itself, I began to change my interpretation of the Two of Swords for that particular deck of mine. I amazed people when I saw the accident in their past, and if it was in the future position, you'd better believe I advised them to wear a seat belt and drive very cautiously!

In the case of symbols evolving over time through experience, you will need to get enough feedback from yourself to know that you are wrong when you are wrong. But take care, when reading for others, not to use feedback in order to generate your readings before or during interpretation. You may inadvertently become a cold reader.

Using the Crystal Ball for Meditation

When I was a very small child, perhaps about four years old, I was at home, playing as usual and spending time with my father and mother, when I was suddenly overcome with a very strange feeling. Up until that point in my life, my body had shuttled my mind around and the two were inextricably bound. But suddenly, with a very uncomfortable sensation, my vision was of my own body sitting where I had been playing, with a glassy-eyed stare. My sight seemed unnatural and I could see my parents in the kitchen, outside of the line of sight of my body. I floated above myself, terrified, before slipping abruptly back into my body as quickly as it had started. Once reunited with my familiar form, I started wailing and crying with the instinctual fear of a child who thinks she has almost died.

My mother came to me right away and held me, asking me what was the matter. I frantically tried to explain that I had just been floating above my own body. I told her that it felt really weird, but that I wasn't hurt. My mother comforted me by telling me I had just had my first out-of-body experience, and that it was a natural thing that happened to her, too. Later I was to learn that out-of-body experiences can be created and controlled through meditation.

How I Learned to Meditate

Meditation was one practice that did not come easily or naturally to me. As a hyperactive child with an incredibly short attention span, I grew up in the era when teachers would demand that misbehaving youth be placed on medication. In fact, I had to leave private school and transfer to public education due to a complete inability to remain on-task.

In my spiritual studies as a teenager, I repeatedly ran across information that convinced me that meditation was not only a physically and emotionally healthy practice, but also very necessary for me to be able to advance my divination and scrying abilities. Reluctantly, I set about the task of attempting to attain the proficiency of a Buddhist monk. To that end, I must admit I have not yet succeeded, but if I can manage to meditate to a moderately effective degree, then anyone can.

I started out frustrated. Following all advice, I stowed myself away in the bedroom in my parents' house, tossing out the cat and turning off the television and music. I lit candles and attempted to focus on my breathing, which seemed to do more harm than good. I was far too concerned with trying to make sure I wasn't "cheating" at slow, square breathing, by taking longer breaths out than breaths in. Simultaneously, I somehow was able to fill my brain with all my troubles with school, parents, and boys despite focusing on my breathing and heart rate, which all the literature had claimed would work. During my first meditation session, I probably didn't even manage ten seconds of a clear mind.

I probably didn't attempt it again for quite some time, but I returned to meditation with determination. For me, it helped to practice breathing without getting angry at myself for not being fully able to clear my mind. That way, I could get into the rhythm of the breaths, which would naturally relax my body and make the performance of the feat of breathing in a particular way less frustrating. True, that took away a lot of the benefit of allowing the breath to be a distraction from daily thought, but it was necessary for me.

After that, allowing my nervous energy to relax and my brain to stop screaming at me just took time and repetition. I remember glancing at a clock each time I thought

I had reached an especially long plateau of calmness, only to be shocked that only a minute or two had passed. Even though it seemed like no progress was being made in my subjective experience of meditation, objectively I did notice with pride that the clock seemed to be moving faster during each successive meditation session.

Once I added visualization to my meditation for grounding purposes, the process suddenly became much easier. But I'm glad that I started out the hard way, because otherwise I would still be unable to clear my mind for more than a few seconds. However, focusing on images such as a tree or colorful balls of light inside me was much more pleasantly distracting from my everyday thoughts than attempting to make the act of breathing a challenge.

How to Meditate with the Ball

Meditation can be a very healthy daily practice, the goal of which is to control your own brain-wave frequency to slip out of a heightened state of stressful alertness, and into the restful frequencies associated with a near-sleep state. It is during this most peaceful trance that you can begin to allow other perceptions into your mind, if you wish for that to happen.

Anyone who knows me can tell you that I am the most attention deficit hyperactivity disorder–type person they know, so if I can meditate, I swear that you can, too. Begin by setting aside a time for meditation. If you've had trouble with meditation before, you can start with a couple minutes, or even thirty seconds. You can always build your-self up to a longer time later when it feels more easy and even pleasurable. But if you set a high goal for yourself and make yourself have a showdown stand-off with your own brain, you're missing the point.

Go to a quiet place where you won't be disturbed. The lighting and temperature should be very comfortable, and you should be in a position that won't distract you. Begin by leaving your crystal in a stand where you can view it, so that if you fall asleep it won't fall out of your hand onto the floor. Once you've learned to control your trance state, you can hold it in either or both hands. If you are new to medi-tation, you may wish to begin by keeping your eyes closed, but the eventual goal is to keep an unfocused gaze on the crystal. Ground yourself thoroughly before beginning your meditation.

Familiarizing yourself with your body's chi through visualization is helpful to bring yourself into a meditative state and may aid chi flow within the crystal as well dur-ing scrying. Pay attention to all areas of your body while you're meditating or scrying, and note any changes that you experience with your energy level or your mind's-eye visualization with respect to your body. Later on, during scrying interpretation, you will be working with symbols, so as you sink into the trance realm, you can begin famil-iarizing yourself with your own body as a symbol before exploring symbols within your internal realm and the external world.

In a way, your own body is where those two realms meet: the internal and the external, the psychological and the physical, the spiritual and the mundane.

Chakras are an internal system of visualizing colorful chi centers that many people use. Though internal energies and colors will be discussed a little bit later with respect to auras and colors, there is much that can and has been written about chakras. For the purposes of this book, I will draw your attention only to a few common ideas that may be useful during your meditation and scrying.

Within your body, just behind the center of your forehead, is the third eye. Some people may feel or imagine this on the skin of the forehead, or even just in front of the forehead. Before psychic work, many readers take time to open the third eye by turning their attention to that area and visualizing color or movement of chi there in order to make sure that they are able to receive information. Rather than this chakra, some people open the chakra near the solar plexus or just above the belly button. This area can also be associated with psychic ability and feeling out the world around you with your intuition.

Before scrying for another person, two other chakras can be opened. One is the heart chakra. Tuning into this area of your body can allow you to love yourself as well as others, and can make it easier for you to open the third eye. The last one of great import in this context is the throat chakra, which can be opened to help you give voice to what you see in the crystal ball to communicate the message to another person.

Breathe deeply and slowly. Listen to your own heart-beat, if you can, and attempt square breathing to the rhythm of your heartbeats. Square breathing is slowly inhaling for four counts, holding your breath for four counts, slowly exhaling for four counts, and then holding again for four counts. Repeat this as long as you need to in order to do it without consciously having to think about what you're doing.

This is the hardest part, but you must clear your mind. Yes, even of the thought of clearing your mind. As thoughts arise, as they naturally will, dismiss them as if you are an outside observer of your own thought processes, and the thoughts are harmlessly floating by as if they belong to somebody else. If you make this a daily practice over time, you will find health benefits happening in your own life in the form of reduced stress levels, better sleep, and more restfulness, and you will find yourself more easily slipping into this trance state for longer periods of time.

Be careful to not get caught up in an analysis of what is internal and what is external. It is natural when you begin to feel thoughts arise that don't seem to be your own, or that seem to have been generated organically from your meditative state, to feel excited and to try to pick them apart immediately. As you begin, I encourage you to slow this process down as much as possible. Remember, you're trying to be without any thoughts at all, so keep allow-ing them to pass by unnoticed. Return to working with your eyes closed if gazing into your crystal increases these thoughts.

Wanting to know what is real and what is unreal is a natural desire, especially if you're like me and experience visions and other perceptions in everyday waking life. I like to think of it in a metaphor, as if I am swimming in an ocean of symbols and the surreal. You can poke your head up above the water and interact with the daily world or you can dunk your head underwater entirely, but you can never quite walk on the land free of all of your perception tinting what you know.

I want you to allow yourself to be fully immersed in this sea. Only then can you learn this foreign language of symbols so that you can fluently convey the messages it has for you. This is the very reason that crystal ball gazing can be so valuable, because when you focus on the crystal, you are given a window into that other world where everything is accepted to be mysterious.

In time, some of you may wish to use crystal ball meditation for trance journeying. For the purposes of this book, I'm going to continue to call journeying in the mind to realms that don't exist on this planet *astral travel*, while journeying in the mind to real places on Earth through an out-of-body experience I'll call *ethereal travel*. (For more on both terms, please see chapter 3.)

Astral travel is an inner world made up entirely of your subconscious. You have control over this world, but you can also work out problems by experiencing things within it.

Astral travel can be like a lucid-dreaming state, in which you are aware that you are not in the real world, but you work within it as if you are having a real experience. Astral travel can begin as simply as allowing yourself to visualize a door in the room, perhaps in the floor or any surface you wish on which there is not actually a real door, and then passing through it in your mind's eye and allowing your imagination to furnish you with the landscape you need. Sometimes people or animals may speak with you on your astral plane, or you may ask them to go away if you do not wish to converse with them or are not ready for that.

Some people work to foster relationships with the people or animals seen during astral travel, believing them to be spirit guides or angels. Spirit guides are thought to be higher beings, or representations of your own higher self, that can communicate information directly to you. You can bypass scrying altogether and use your crystal ball to communicate messages from your spirit guides, and many people do.

In addition to spirit guides and angels, you may find yourself connecting with a personification of that particular crystal ball itself. This can be a good way for you to develop a rapport with the particular crystal ball you are using, as well as to internalize the crystal ball's chi and fully integrate it with your own subconscious in order to feel more comfortable reading and to benefit from any additional properties of the crystal you chose.

The crystal ball can be a valuable first link to spirit guides that can later be contacted with or without use of the crystal to perform psychic readings without scrying. However, spirit guides are not required for meditation, scrying, or any psychic work, so if you don't believe in them or are unable to work with them at this time in your life, you don't have to do so.

Another valuable trance practice is *automatic writing*. Get a pad of paper and a pen and allow yourself to sit in trance for some time until you feel assured that you are dropped deep into nearly a stage of sleep, where your mind is clear. Allow your hand to move on the paper, but do not look at or focus your eyes on the writing. Practice until you are not thinking at all about words or language so that your writing is performed in a complete trance. It is better to have illegible loops than words that you thought up. Do not read the writing until after you are fully complete with your meditative session.

After your allotted time of meditation and automatic writing is complete, please remember to ground yourself again, especially if you feel lightheaded or a have a head-ache. As I mentioned previously, eating some food, putting a little salt on your tongue, or holding a piece of hematite can help you ground more quickly and thoroughly if you are unfamiliar with grounding or had a particularly intense session.

When you begin the process of analysis, it can be very challenging. Keep a notebook in which you can transcribe your trance handwriting into something legible. Write in your journal any insights about the written words that may arise. If there are symbols or repeated words or phrases, tally these in your notebook and write about any meanings that they give to you at the time. You can sit in meditation on those symbols, words, or phrases later on if you'd like to continue working on puzzling out their interpretation for you.

six

Special Considerations When Reading for Others

A client once came to me asking for a reading to describe her future husband. I started out by explaining to her that ultimately she would be responsible for choosing or not choosing to pursue prospective suitors, but that I would be glad to perform a reading to look for a compatible match. As we sat down together, I began to get some very clear descriptors that were associated with a specific person. Now, I actually tend to get a little worried when I only see one person as a potential match. Some clients feel a lot of pressure when they aren't given many choices right off the bat! I saw a chubby gentleman with dark skin who sat comfortably in a uniform. I also saw a guitar. So I let this client know about this physical description, along with the symbols that indicated a military career and playing an instrument in the past.

After I ran through the entire reading, happily enough the client said that description described her current boyfriend perfectly! My client felt more at ease knowing that she and her boyfriend would be compatible for marriage, if that was their eventual choice. A few months later, I received an e-mail asking me for my address so that she could send me an invitation to their wedding since they had set a date!

How I Learned to Read the Crystal Ball for Others

I started off reading for friends at school as a child, but the crystal ball showed its real strengths when I became an adult and started my own business. The teenagers I'd been reading for preferred tarot cards as a mode of divination, because they each had a deck and were reading along with the instruction books so that they could feel informed. As a result, I became accustomed to reading for others, usually through other means. It was absolutely trial and error when I first started reading for others, because I had to understand their needs from the reading when previously I only had concern with my own. Suddenly, I had to carefully tiptoe around certain subjects or even refuse to read for people entirely, and it took time for me to realize that was okay.

In one instance, a woman came to me with what would become a fairly regular problem, which was that she thought her boyfriend was cheating on her. She asked me if I could provide her with a reading that would definitively tell her that he was cheating, and whether or not it was time for her to end things with the man she loves. Offhandedly, she mentioned that she had already been to several psychics, and each had told her that he was cheating on her, but there had been differences in opinions between the professionals as to whether she should leave him or not.

Her revelation about the other psychics caused me to put the brakes on her reading and dig a little deeper. Why, I pondered, would she waffle so much for so long on her decision as to whether to leave him if she was absolutely sure he was cheating? When gently pressed, she finally confided in me that the reasons she was stuck in this continuous loop, seeking readings on the same subject, was that she felt she couldn't act on the advice. "I can't tell him, 'My psychic told me you were cheating,'" she lamented. "He would think I was crazy."

I did not choose to read for that particular client on that day. I pointed out that another reading, no matter what its content, would not make her decision any easier to carry out. She unequivocally stated that, at that point in time, she had chosen to stay with her boyfriend. Even though she knew about his cheating ways, and no further reading from me was going to make the necessary confrontation for her own health any less uncomfortable, I invited her to come back for a reading anytime that she was ready for guidance through the next stage in her life.

Dipping my toes into the world of charging money started when I went off to college. I began at a fundraiser for a student group, which was delightful because it allowed me to see that the value of my work could be represented in real money, while not making me feel nervous that I was charging for readings even though I wasn't the best reader in the world. I automatically reached for my tarot cards for each of my new clients, who were mostly fraternity boys asking questions about girls and staff members asking questions about ex-husbands.

I was just starting to get into the rhythm of things when a young man about my age approached with an older friend and simply asked me how his dad was. I didn't have to be a psychic to know that his father was recently deceased. The pain in his eyes was too raw and fresh. This level of intimacy suddenly seemed very out of place in the sunlit student building filled with laughter and bustling crowds.

For some reason, I felt that tarot cards wouldn't be enough for this guy. A stranger, probably new to divination, didn't need wisdom from the riddles of pictures drawn on paper, but wanted confirmation of things that he knew about his father. I paused to retrieve a crystal ball from my backpack before proceeding. As the young man in front of me fought back tears, I began with a physical description of the man who appeared in the crystal. I then relayed messages from the man in the crystal, which came both as what seemed like sounds to my ears as well as a series of pictures, some of which appeared as symbols that I could puzzle out but others that I simply described to my young client while he nodded knowingly with surprised eyes. After the reading had ended, he thanked me profusely and then left. His friend thanked me even more.

It still often surprises me when I elicit tears from strangers, but it happens more often with the crystal ball than with any other tool, simply due to the visual imagery that can be described to match another person's memory exactly. More recently, I performed a reading for an older woman who nonchalantly asked about her father. We were both on camera, as I was recording the reading for marketing and research purposes as well as self-improvement. She seemed comfortable asking about her father, and now that I'm more experienced I made sure to ask whether she was sure that she was ready to hear things that might be good or bad. She was almost dismissive in her eagerness to get on with the reading and appeared relaxed and cheerful.

As I began to describe a man, a car, and a summer home out in the woods, more and more details seemed to pour through the crystal ball. I not only described the subtle nuances of the pictures I saw, such as the height and placement of the trees relative to the roof of the cabin-like home, but also pondered aloud what the symbolic meaning might be of a building shrouded by trees, even though the pictures seemed detailed and vivid enough to be real places and things. I did not get a verbal response from my client, so I continued with my eyes fixated on the crystal.

After the reading, she appeared to have been very moved and told me that I had described a home of hers as well as confirming other details. When I played back the recorded video, I was surprised to see that she had to wipe away tears during her reading, and I felt honored that I had been able to participate in that moment in her life.

After her reading, this client was also profoundly thankful, feeling that I had been drawn into her life for this very purpose. Reading for others with the crystal ball is an incredibly rewarding experience simply because of the gratitude received. At times, I have felt that a reading wasn't going well because the images shown in the crystal ball were new to me and seemed like random objects that would have no meaning to anyone: a pair of sunglasses, a man shoveling manure. I'd struggle to find metaphorical meaning in the moment, hoping clients wouldn't think I was just naming things I'd seen earlier that day, only to find out after the reading that each symbol had seized the other person immediately with an important and direct meaning.

On another occasion I was working in a tent at a city fair, having fun entertaining the children with their parents and also sending them home with the curious zing of truth to give them that sense of wonderment. It was hardly the usual setting for a séance. When a couple approached me and handed me the money for a reading regarding the woman's dead brother, I explained to them that, ideally, I would like to have a private appointment to fully explore the matter. Crestfallen, the woman explained that they had been fans of mine for a very long time from a distance, and had seen this event of mine and traveled quite a ways just to see me. Deeply concerned, the woman explained that her mother felt that witchcraft had killed her brother.

Effective deadly witchcraft is highly improbable, especially in this country, but since I do believe it to be possible, I agreed to do a reading so that, if any negative witchcraft were discovered, I could work against it. The crystal ball I brought to the fair was smaller for ease of travel. I rested the two-and-a-half-inch orb in my palm and dropped into a light trance state to scry, while keeping my awareness of the bustling festival around me.

Images flooded the crystal fairly early on. Among them, I saw a man, maybe in his thirties, lying next to a swimming pool, an empty liquor bottle by his hand. Then I saw an image of him stumbling through a house. I did see some occult symbols, as if he may have had some of those images around him. However, there were no indications that any spell work had been used against him. I finished up the reading, making certain that this was the case.

I told the client that there seemed to have been substance abuse involved in the death. Though I felt the occult symbolism was interesting, I confirmed for her that there was no witchcraft involved in his death and that everyone was safe in that regard. At this point, the client said something that surprised me. She told me that her brother had been a very young child, around the age of three. Almost at once, I offered her the money back, saying, "I did not see that at all." When calling upon the dead, I do not force one person to come through, so occasionally other spirits arrive that surprise even me. Since I did not see the boy, I assumed that was what had occurred.

Not even attempting to take the money back from my hand, she shook her head and both she and her boyfriend agreed that I had been right on. A couple who were both addicted to drugs had been caretakers of the boy when he died by drowning in a swimming pool. My clients were relieved enough to find that witchcraft was not the culprit. Other people's feedback and reactions to the images seen in the crystal ball are very rewarding instant gratification for the reader.

I very recently received an e-mail from a man for whom I had performed a love reading nine months ago, before he met the love of his life. He let me know that he is now engaged to a woman whom I'd described perfectly. Her personality and physical traits matched. I had even told him that she would be deaf. He was extremely happy, but I didn't get a wedding invitation this time around.

One woman I read for at a fair for "Women of Wisdom" did not yet look visibly pregnant, but after her reading revealed a baby, she told me that she already knew. She was so charmed with my physical description and story about the day of her baby's birth that she later told me that she had chosen to name her child after me. This was certainly an incredible honor and a high point in my career.

If you want to read for people other than your friends and family, and you don't have access to a group that is willing to use you in a fundraiser, there are many psychic fairs located all over the world that welcome newcomers. Indeed, this is one way that I continued my learning when I chose to read for strangers, before I was able to build a private client base. I simply looked around at local meta-physical bookstores and online for psychic fairs, spiritual events, and even city fairs that allowed vendors to purchase a booth space for a fee and then interact with the public. I found these experiences highly valuable for a long period of time, but also with distinct challenges for crystal ball readers.

Just planning the logistics of the event can be a hassle. Paying a hefty booth fee, parking, and setting up a heavy booth, table, and three chairs for myself and a couple of clients was always an annoyance. Transporting a crystal ball without breaking it is something of which we crystal ball readers must always be mindful. Getting food and drink as well as using the lavatory can be difficult, since a crystal ball looks valuable and can be stolen by strangers at a fair. I learned to make friends with the person in the booth next to mine, so that we could keep an eye out for each other, or simply to pack my valuable crystal on my person wherever I went.

In my very first forays into reading the crystal ball for strangers at fairs, I was surprised to find that some other readers were not friendly to me. There is strong competition in my region, and so, to this day, I am especially friendly to other readers I see reading for the public, even if I am not vending at the same fair. Do not be discouraged by those who see you as a threat. Because I was a young eighteen-year-old when I started out, others were leery of trusting their secrets or money to somebody who looked like a kid. As I write these words, I am twenty-nine years of age, and when reading in public next to an elderly reader who has less experience than I do, the public may still choose her due to her appearance of wisdom. Don't be discouraged by that, if you happen to be young. Know that there truly is wisdom that comes with age and experience, regardless of crystal ball reading skill, and that you too will continue to improve and earn respect as you become older.

Self-Care

Pay attention to your own self-care, especially when performing readings for others. If you do more than one reading in a day, make sure you're still grounding properly, reading barefoot, and paying attention to what your body is telling you to decide whether you need a break or to stop for the day. For those of you who are professionals in another form of divination or are working toward becoming professional crystal ball readers, know that I think that this is the best job on earth but possibly also one with the highest turnover.

I like to joke that I never perform a reading when I have a hangover because all that I would predict is blinding pain. There is a kernel of truth there. Listen to your body, because doing readings can feel like it takes more out of you than other seated activities that don't take as much brain power and energy.

Interpreting What You See and How to Relay It to the Other Person

Interpret in the same way that you would for yourself. The other person may add his or her own insights afterward, or even without telling you, and that's okay. You need only be aware of relating to the other person sensitively. If a person seeking a reading is coming from a negative place of fear, that can affect whether the reading will be a positive experience. The person asking for a reading should ideally be relaxed and resolved to seek information to make choices that will change his or her life. If the person is already confident in his or her decisions and is coming from a combative place, a reading may not be necessary at all. If a person has just suffered a loss and wants to know if her loved one is "okay" on the other side, but would be devastated if there were any indication that her loved one was not okay, a reading should be postponed until the person is further along in the grieving process.

When I began to read for others, I was amused at the stereotypes people expected and the myths they held about crystal ball reading, such as "Are you going to tell me when I'm going to die?" My own father thought that he would die at age forty-two because a fortuneteller told him so. Incidentally, she was two decades off. He died at age sixty-two after battling cancer. Some people feel that there's nowhere else to go, to talk about this thing that will happen at the end of every life, but to a crystal ball reader. For most people, it is merely a morbid curiosity, springing forth from the deeper need to talk about death. Even children will ask this question, when they are far away from their own death.

I don't think that these questions should be automatically glossed over. Their importance is great, especially since the client asking may not feel that he or she has anyone else that can be consulted about the realm of death. Again, these questions are those that may need some gentle rephrasing, since we can obviously play a major role with our choices in pushing out or speeding up the date of our deaths. Knowing a projected date is not helpful to most people, unless it is a person already dealing with end-of-life issues who is making specific plans for his or her affairs.

As a community chaplain at Harborview Medical Center and the University of Washington Medical Center in Seattle, I've worked with many people who are dealing with very practical issues in their last days and wishing for a timeline. Find out exactly why your client is exploring end-of-life issues at this time so that you can rephrase the questions accordingly. Perhaps you will ask your crystal, "What sort of red-flag situations should be avoided in order to protect this client from the possibility of accidental death?"

I've also had the unfortunate experience many times of being told by somebody else that he or she felt like choosing death over life. It can be very sad when you have a person in front of you who wants your help and you know you cannot help him or her. However, take some joy and pride in the fact that this person chose to share this with you. You are the first person who is trusted to bring proper help to the situation. In a sense, you get to act as a guardian angel, or a key to recovery from a terrible situation.

As a beginner, I laughed at how people were so frightened that I was going to instantly look for something bad and predict grave danger, just like in the movies. I was happy to give people an experience that went against those stereotypes. Others seemed to embrace a misunderstanding of what it was that I do, and I had to more gently dissuade them.

Health Readings

I am asked very often for health readings, and by far the most common question coming from women is whether or not they are pregnant. The second-most common client question comes from people desperate to find a diagnosis for a perceived health problem. The first time that this happened to me, I was rather surprised by it. I hadn't asked the crystal ball any health questions for myself yet, having been a relatively healthy youth, and so I simply asked the crystal ball about whether a skin problem of a strange client was important or not. At the time, I saw images of foods that I assumed might point to an allergy, so I cheerfully gave my guess. When I told a friend about the reading afterward, she terrified me by telling me that the person might die of some kind of skin cancer if I were wrong and then their family could come to sue me for all I was worth.

Health readings, if done improperly, may also leave the reader legally liable for damages that happen to the client and his or her family, if any of these negative things were to occur due to delay of proper medical treatment. I would advise a beginner to completely avoid doing health readings for strangers, and be very cautious even about doing them for oneself. People who cannot afford health care can be referred to social workers, found in many hospitals, who have access to a myriad of resources to get those bills paid or waived. In the United States, departments of Social and Health Services in each state also have social workers to help clients apply for financial aid either before or after treatment and billing has taken place.

When Not to Read

You shouldn't read for someone who seems to perceive that what you do is give advice that is best given by another professional, such as a doctor, lawyer, or financial advisor. Readings on financial or legal topics can be used by some clients to procrastinate, so it is important to realize that just because you are asked to read on a particular topic doesn't mean that you are forced to address it or that it is even the most important topic to address.

You can also avoid getting into trouble by obtaining parental permission before you tell the fortunes of children. If you take your crystal ball to a kids' birthday party, for example, you can have permission slips sent home ahead of time. Fortunetelling for children is a wonderful thing, and they are especially delighted to play a part in interpreting the symbols that you see. Of course, you must take special care not to be as blunt as you might be with an adult who is able to bear bad news. If you see a child's parents dying, for example, please don't spoil the party by telling the child. Reading for kids in most cases is quite fun for all involved.

Another situation in which you might postpone a reading is when someone asks the same question over and over, even after having received an answer from a reading. This can happen for several reasons. Some people may not be satisfied until they get the answer they want to hear. But more innocently, it can happen when somebody just wants to check, especially when done with several different readers, just to make sure the answer is absolutely certain.

The grass can always seem greener on the other side, and many people just want to hear about a situation that is very different from their own, but one that they would never actually choose. For example, a happily married but bored woman might want many readings on whether people outside her marriage are attracted to her, even though she is not actually planning on pursuing anyone. Somebody who has a very stressful job may want readings on what it would be like to start their own knitting business even if that's not something practical that they'd ever do. There's nothing wrong with wanting to be wanted, or with needing a fantasy escape, but, in these cases, the readings would be treating a symptom rather than a cause. This can be bad for you as a reader as well, since painting such a picture that is opposite but appealing is a cold-reading tactic.

(I'll have more to say about cold reading a bit later in this chapter.)

Don't get me wrong, you will be helping the other person make choices, and some of them will be difficult and vastly different from the choices he or she has made in the past. As you can see, the danger isn't exactly in a specific topic or quantity of readings for an individual, but rather, in the way that the person is using the readings. One philosophical issue has to do with our Western culture, in which freedom is valued to the point that, ironically, it is paralyzing.

People are held hostage by the illusion of choice. Back in the old days, there were fewer choices to be made in life. Women often knew that they would grow up to raise a family. Men often knew that they would eventually take on the same work as their fathers. In modern times, depression can arise when one does not achieve an alternate goal. Even when choices are firmly made, comparisons are made to the other life that could have been chosen, making every choice seem not ideal. Surely the grass is always greener on the other side.

Part of the service you will provide, as a reader, is not only in pointing out the many choices, but also in helping the other person evaluate them. This can feel uncomfortable, as it will smack of judging, and many are not familiar or confident with judging the lives of others. Realize that your judgments will naturally come from a place of your own filters of culture and experience, and are thus analytical but should still be informed by your intuition.

For example, a reading from the crystal ball might reveal that, if a woman waited for her deadbeat boyfriend to call, she might next experience love and emotional intimacy in ten years. But if she left her boyfriend, she could find deeper love and emotional intimacy in ten months. Obviously, it is ultimately up to her to decide whether she feels this boyfriend is worth it. However, chances are that many people will turn to you and ask you for your opinion. It is all right to admit that you feel she deserves to find better love and sooner to boot. Be sure to make it clear, though, that the difference between what you've seen in the crystal and what your personal opinion is, is based upon your experience. It is only fair and ethical to allow adults to make choices, even when you are very certain that they are the wrong ones.

It is my belief that the future can be changed, and that, in fact, is the entire point of getting readings. If the answers were outcomes written in stone, a reading would be a fun and scary party trick, but it would not be very helpful for a person trying to make life choices. We are each in charge of our own destinies, but we work within a framework of possibilities. It is the purpose of divination to discover and evaluate those potentials.

When you measure anything in life, you change it. That's the famous Heisenberg uncertainty principle at work. For example, if you stick a thermometer into a hot glass of water, you change the temperature of the water, if only very slightly. As you begin to make conscious or unconscious decisions about how to move forward as you receive a reading, it is natural that your next reading may already reflect your intentions. It is important to wait until you have firmly made your decisions in life and moved on to the next ones at hand before you elect to perform or receive another reading.

The last thing you should be aware of before performing a reading for yourself or for another is to listen to your intuition if it tells you that it is a bad time for a reading. If there is an indicator that you should not read, whether it be a simple answer of "no" using divination to ask if it is a right time for a reading or a very reluctant spirit with which you are unable to conduct clear communication, it may be time to call it quits. If you are working with another person, even a paying client, he or she would appreciate an honest refund or an appointment rescheduled than a reading turned into a negative experience.

Regarding permission for readings, it is often said that it is not right to read anyone without their explicit permission. For those of us who can't "turn off" our talents, this may go a bit too far. After all, for those who believe in chi, natural reading is done by everyone during everyday conversations as our auras interact with those of others. However, once you communicate the content of your readings to another, you've crossed a boundary. This may feel like a natural extension of marketing for some professional readers, as pointing out to somebody on the street that they have a new love coming into their life soon and handing over a business card can be a way to get speedy appointments made. To others, it may seem like you are compelled to do this work in everyday life, especially if you see danger or even death in a person's future and feel as though it is your duty to warn that person.

However, it is never your duty to force a reading onto an unsuspecting person, and doing a reading without being asked is tacky at best. As explained earlier, there are many people who cannot and will not use readings correctly and positively in their lives, or simply do not wish to. It is wrong to force information gained from a reading onto somebody against his or her will. If you are to do work with a family on a reading, make sure that the family comes to you first and requests your service. Volunteering out of the blue, even with good intentions, can seem like extortion to a desperate family and hinder their own grieving process more than it can help.

If, as a beginner, you have high energy and feel like you could do hundreds of readings a day at any price, and you gain confidence in your readings and love for your readings, it will also be easy for you to want to spread the word, almost like a missionary—reading for anyone who will listen to your voice. It is true that you are now an ambassador for this art, if you choose to read for others. However, if you encounter others with ideological differences, it is best to hold off on a reading, for their own benefit or at least to be very honest about what you can and cannot do. If you don't believe in angels or soul mates, you may not meet some clients' expectations, which can lead to anger and dissatisfaction reflecting poorly on you and the practice as a whole.

How to Deal with Criticism

How do you make the crystal ball seem valid to skeptics who find it hokey? The short answer is that you don't. Crystal ball reading is not a gospel to be spread, and even if you are getting wonderful results that have changed your life for the better, having those results won't necessarily cause everyone to take action to make their lives better. Any reader who chooses to read for others can become what my husband terms "an emotional dumping ground." So, it is important to realize that you can refuse service to those who you know will not have a positive reading experience with you, even if they are close friends and family, or are willing to pay you money.

When I first began reading for others, I was surprised at the assumption by many others that I was just looking for an unsuspecting rube to "cross my palm with silver" and make money without performing a service. A couple of months ago, a visitor to my website posted a comment on my reviews page, where clients can post their ratings and feedback about my readings. A visiting stranger went to that page and wrote that the reviews were all "obviously fake." At the time, I was rather tickled by the idea that somebody out there thought my reviews were too good to be true! I told my best friend and my husband, and we all had a chuckle. A classic misconception of a crystal ball reader is that he or she is running some sort of scam, often involving witchcraft or an evil curse.

This idea is so prevalent that I was rejected as being "too controversial" by a local program during the winter here in Washington state called "Waste Free Holidays." The slogan was "Give experiences instead of stuff," and King County Waste Management allowed local businesses that provided such experiences to donate coupons so that more consumers would buy gift certificates instead of cluttering up landfills with bulky gifts and wrapping paper. Misconceptions can indeed cause controversy.

I even had an extremely difficult time trying to get a credit-card processing company to accept my business. I went through my bank, however, and my bank went to their third-party merchant vendor in Texas, which balked at finding out that I was a fortuneteller. My spooky money, good enough for the government to tax, was not good enough for them. My money was also refused by a local advertising agency with a small newsletter franchise. The owner claimed that she was worried that other advertisers would not want to have their ad seen on the same page as mine, and thus she would lose much more money overall. The classic idea of the old lady throwing curses at people wasn't one she wanted next to coupons for an oil change.

Here's how I run things, and I recommend this model: first of all, I don't ever look purposely for negativity or evil magic in somebody's reading. That falls under the idea that I should always ask permission before reading for somebody. Just as I wouldn't walk up to somebody on the street and announce that he or he was going to die the next day, I wouldn't start talking about a curse affecting health problems if a person came in asking about his or her work or love life. When reading for somebody else, the other person should always be in charge of the reading process from the beginning.

A client will often come in and specifically ask whether he or she is cursed. And yes, I do mean *often*. My personal belief system does include a belief in curses, so I do regard it as a possibility, but my experience has also left me with a great degree of skepticism in the majority of cases. You see, nearly every day that I work I get asked by at least one person whether he or she has a curse. However, in over a decade of working with the crystal ball, I have only seen two legitimate cases of a curse. In both cases, the person cursed had been steeped in another culture that uses curses more often. One was a Native American from a reservation who had some bad blood with members of his tribe. The other had spent time outside of the country in an area in which curses are used in everyday life. For both of these people, I offered to remove the curses free of charge. Both accepted, and one even handed me an envelope of money afterward, which I did accept.

In my belief system, curses can be removed in most cases through simple prayer, so I instruct clients how to do that before I offer to remove it myself for free in addition to their efforts. The same model can be used if you offer spiritual healing or other spell work that others might assume you provide along with crystal ball reading, especially love spells. In my opinion, it is unwise to charge money to remove a curse without providing a free alternative. Even if you are well-meaning, you must understand that even in true cases of curses this can seem like extortion. A cursed person may feel as though he or she has no other way out than to pay you. And in a world where, ostensibly, no magic exists, you can obviously be accused of fraud. It's also just not a very nice place in which to put another person. He or she feels an obligation to buy from you rather than feeling empowered.

Cold Reading

The last, but certainly not least, of the additional challenge of reading for other people as opposed to just yourself is accidentally cold reading, which is an easy mistake for new crystal ball readers to make. Cold reading, as I've mentioned, is the art of appearing to perceive more information from a person than you do. Mentalists can use cold-reading techniques to trick even very intelligent, educated, and wise audience participants. Unfortunately, some of the most common cold-reading techniques can accidentally be used by genuine readers, especially as beginners, since they get such positive feedback when the techniques are used. For the benefit of others and yourself, as a reader, it is important to avoid cold-reading techniques whenever possible.

The first and easiest way to prevent accidental cold reading is to minimize information exchange before and during the reading. I do like to allow other people to be able to ask questions of my crystal ball; however, I want it to remain optional. It is all right to ask if the client has a topic of focus or a question that he or she would like answered, but if the client would like to keep it private, that should be that person's prerogative. If you are a skeptical reader yourself, you can certainly launch into reading without using a specific question.

It is also easy to accidentally elicit too much feedback during the reading. I tend to talk very fast, as do many readers, so it was easy for me as a beginner to keep asking the client whether he or she understood: "Does that make sense?" The intention is only clarity. But with each answer the client gives, it may subconsciously or consciously alter the course of your reading away from where you were being guided by the crystal. If you have the same problem, I suggest that, before the reading, you explain to the other person that you will be going very fast without asking for feedback. Tell your client that there can be time after you've gone through what you've needed to say for clarifying questions to be asked, or that he or she is welcome to stop you at any time if none of it is making any sense.

It is a misconception that body language is a major form of cold reading, so you don't have to worry about people keeping a poker face. Though you'll want to avoid forcing them to nod or shake their heads, chances are that you will have your eyes on your crystal most of the time. It is also a myth that cold readers use a lot of Sherlock Holmes–style deduction.

However, if you find yourself analytically thinking about the other person's appearance or any other external stimuli, gently remind yourself to keep in a light trance and turn your focus more inward. Making suppositions of a person's focus in life due to age is something we do naturally in everyday life, and when used in cold reading it is an example of a *Jacques statement*. It can be easy to begin talking about reflection upon life in times of retirement if speaking with an older person, or the trouble of finding somebody who shares your passion if speaking with a young person.

It is hard to move away from these perfectly natural assumptions, so don't think that you're immune. Sometimes the intellectual strain of organizing a crystal ball reading can even make you more susceptible. For example, if you normally have good "gaydar" in your everyday life, but when reading always start asking the crystal about someone of the opposite sex of the person with whom you're sitting, you're making an assumption based on your culture and your mental state rather than on your intuition.

The second most common cold-reading technique that I see accidentally used by genuine and well-meaning readers is the *rainbow ruse*. With this technique, two opposite statements are made at the same time so that the person must fall somewhere along the spectrum—for example, "You are a very generous and helpful person, but even you have a selfish streak that rears its ugly head at times." Of course the other person will find at least one of these conditions true, as the statement covers all cases of selfishness and selflessness. The rainbow ruse has become so common in part because symbol-interpretation books include two aspects to the same symbol that reflect both positive and negative aspects of the symbol.

I found that I was especially susceptible to this when I was first reading reversals or upside-down symbols. Many of the traditional interpretations are quite opposite reflections of the right-side-up symbol. The beginner might nervously blur the lines, covering both bases by stating the right-side-up meaning as well as the upside-down, creating perfect rainbow ruse statements every time. Positive reinforcement from those who have been accidentally tricked can further perpetuate this beginner mistake. Take care not to fill your crystal ball dictionary with rainbow ruse statements. It may take longer to learn things the hard way, through trial and error, but it will make you a better reader.

As you work to make your crystal ball dictionary more clearly polarized with its meanings, make sure that you're not tending toward only positive interpretations. We're all suckers for compliments, and this can be a form of cold reading as well.

Take the statement "You are more honest than most people you know" as an example: nobody wants to believe that he or she is more dishonest than 50 percent of other people. Also, it can be easy to assume an interest in personal psychic ability in everybody. Chances are that anyone who comes to a psychic believes in psychic powers and has had experiences of their own. Be careful, though, as this can be another form of flattery that may be undeserved in some people, who are as of yet ignorant of their own potential for psychic talent. It can be easy to fall into the trap of only telling somebody what he or she wants to hear. Make sure that you are teaching yourself how to spot red flags so that you can warn people of negative signs and what to do about them.

Third, make sure that you do not fill your crystal ball dictionary with *Barnum statements*. This cold-reading technique is to make a statement that is so general that it could apply to everyone. For example, "You are intelligent, but much of this is from the school-of-life experience instead of through book knowledge." Wouldn't that statement apply to everyone? It is natural to be conservative when you're a beginner with your readings. Understand that you want to be progressing to more and more precision as you read. Everyone wants details, and though it can be nerve-wracking, pushing yourself to be more precise can also be very rewarding.

Take the case of a man who needs to choose between two women he thinks he loves. Which one does he love more? Which one is most compatible with him? He wants you to confirm a specific answer. In this case, Barnum statements can do more harm than good. If you say something that applies to both women, such as that she is beautiful and captivating, or intelligent or talkative or shy, it may only frustrate the man, who wants to be absolutely sure of his decision. Push yourself to keep looking for identifying details, such as physical characteristics, names, and dates. Your first instinct may be to ask for identifying information so that you can read on each woman. Many readers even automatically ask for birth dates, even though the crystal ball does not require a birth date. Remember, though, that you want to try to work with as little information as possible so as not to accidentally cold read using your intellect instead of doing a real reading with your intuition.

If you know the birth dates, you might make a guess based on age, or you may have some personal associations with the names that might influence you. If the client doesn't volunteer that information, however, I suggest that you avoid asking.

Reading Auras

If you tend to see *auras*, or a layer of color that surrounds a person, either within the crystal ball or even during everyday life, sometimes changes can be telling. For example, if you were performing a crystal ball reading on a man you had just met, and you saw him within the crystal ball with a bright green color surrounding him, you may have an immediate reaction to that color. If you like green, you may have a different reaction than if you think green is the ugliest color in the spectrum. If the image in the crystal ball started growing a red spot in the heart region, that might give you still more meanings. You may have an emotional reaction to the color red, the location of the heart, or even the clashing combination of the two colors together. If the same man came to you the next day and you found that he was entirely surrounded by the color red, that change may be significant to him as well as to you.

It is very common for readers to see people in the crystal ball surrounded by an aura, so if you do not see auras around people in everyday life, and even if you do, it may be beneficial for you to explore the idea of auras. Many people believe that the perception of auras is directly related to the theory that chi, or life energy, exists within all living things. Some people see auras around plants and animals. The belief is that chi should always be moving around and changing. The red flag, so to speak, is when you notice that this flow and change stops or becomes stuck anywhere, which can be an indication of blockages in life or even ill health.

It can be tempting, when a person with known health issues appears with a very abnormal-looking aura, to attempt to alter it back to "normal" yourself by forcing it to conform to what you think it should look like with your mind or even with the laying of hands on the place where you see the aura. Although trained practitioners do this, I'd like to caution beginners against it. First of all, it is hard to know exactly what "normal" is for this particular person. Second, your own health might be affected by this process. Third, even if you force the aura to conform to something better, it would be temporary and may prevent the person from balancing themselves with their own strength of will.

Auras are naturally affected by the proximity of other auras. If you are near someone you like and are having a conversation, your aura will naturally draw near that person's and perhaps even envelop or merge with the other aura as the fields take on some of each other's properties. If you do want to affect another person's aura to improve that person's health, the best way I can recommend is to work on strengthening your own aura, making it look as it looks when you feel healthy and at your best. The other person's aura may mirror your own, allowing the other person to work on achieving that healthy state on his or her own.

If you don't see auras in people outside the crystal ball, there are other tools that can be used. For example, if you do own a pendulum, you can hold it directly over someone and watch its movement as you move away from the body. When the movement changes or stops, it can show the edge at which your perception of the aura ends. You can even sense an aura without tools at all, often by moving your hands near a person without touching him or her and feeling for slight perception changes in temperature, pressure, or texture, such as a fuzzy and warm feeling.

A fun exercise to help you develop your perception of auras can be done with a partner. Sit together facing one another and raise your hands to meet each other, as if you were playing patty-cake. Separate your hands from one another by just a little bit, and then try to slowly move your hands around along the plane between the two of you, so that there is never any less or more space in between your hands. Keep the movement very slow and keep your eyes open, but try to feel the other person even as you are watching for the changes in movement that signal that you are to mirror the movement.

After a time, you can experiment with speeding up the motion and see if that affects your ability to mirror each other's movements. Next, have a third person or a video camera monitor you as you try closing your eyes. Keep close at first and see if you can maintain correct mirrored motion. Then stop and move your seated positions farther away from each other. See how big a distance you can get without losing your ability to mirror each other's motion. You can even try putting a wall in between the two of you and see if you can maintain this connection.

This experience can help you understand auras as more than just a symbolic color, but as a symbolic or even literal way to connect with people without even touching them. This can help you with your remote viewing or ethereal travel, as well as assist you with understanding some external manifestations of what is going on inside a person when you are interpreting auras within the crystal ball.

Colors have even more of the problems that numbers have with interpretation. While some people may not have a favorite number, nearly everyone has a favorite color. Also, while it may be easier to be objective with some symbols, colors often evoke strong emotions. There may be no way you can pretend that you like an ugly color. There's also the likelihood that colors are literally perceived differently by every person. So, the red that you see might be the yellow that the person next to you sees. My first physics teacher joked that one day he was going to write a book called *Your Own Personal Rainbow*, due to the fact that each person sees a different rainbow when waves of light travel to each individual's eyes.

Every culture has meanings for colors, so while people in the West might view the color red as associated with anger, the color red is associated with birth in Japan. The Japanese word for "red" sounds similar to their word for "baby." As with numbers, you may have to rely heavily on lengthy analysis, meditation, and experience before you begin to be really fluent with your language of colors.

Psychologists score color perception in the Rorschach inkblot test as giving direct insight into one's emotional life. So, if you are having a reading in which you see more color than usual, pay attention to the emotions felt during the reading. If you are doing the reading on a client and more colors show, that may indicate that the client's emotional life, relationships, and love should be given more focus. If you always perceive a lot of color in the crystal ball when using it to read on a specific person, it shows that being emotional is a personality trait for that particular person.

One advantage that colors have for interpretation is the ability for you to compare changes almost immediately. Earlier I mentioned that some symbols will gain clarity with experience, as you will see them over and over again. If you tend to see colors, you will see them as aspects in every reading, allowing you to gain experience more quickly. And you may even be able to see shifts and changes within the same reading, and the changes in color will tell you more than the colors would alone.

Example Color	Interpretations
Red	South, fire, Aries, the month of March, Mars, masculine, aggression, action, anger, passionate love. A pur-

plish red can be associated with Cancer or the month of June.

Orange

Masculine, the sun, energy, and
power. Brownish orange can be Scorpio or the month of October.

Yellow

East, air, intellect, knowledge, study,
Sagittarius, or the month of November. A tan color can be Pisces or the
month of February.

Green

North, Virgo, the month of August,
Venus, love, the heart. Growth and
living things. Sexuality, money, Earth,
material things, physical health, feminine.

Blue

West, death, emotional health and
healing, feminine. Libra or Aquarius,
the months of September or January.

Purple

Taurus, Gemini, Leo, the months
of April, May, or July. If dark to the
point of being nearly black, it can be
Capricorn or the month of December
and may also mean protection.

seven

Example Readings

In demonstrating how to put together a reading out of all this practice, I will begin by giving some concrete examples of some of the symbols I might see in a few very specific types of readings. I'll give some theoretical examples of the thought process I might go through during a reading as I interpret or prepare to interpret the symbols. Some topics may need to be approached differently from others. Even though each uses the crystal ball as a tool, our problems don't have cookie-cutter solutions, and likewise your use of the same symbol may be different for different readings.

After several common topics are explored, I'll give examples of notes taken from real crystal ball readings so that you can get an idea of the amount of variation as well as the similarities between them. Although some details have been omitted or slightly changed to maintain the anonymity of the clients involved, each of the symbols given represents the actual context in which I received it during a reading. This can be helpful as you begin to notice patterns in your own readings. Some things that might make you feel frustrated, such as repeated symbols coming up, may be normal. So, if you feel as though your readings aren't going the way that you expected, take a look at my examples, but remember that every reader is different as well.

Money

I've never had a client come to me who didn't wish he or she had more money—and chances are that you could use a bit more of the stuff as well. When I begin a reading on money matters for myself or others, I am always on the lookout for obvious symbols such as coins. The pentacle, a five-pointed star surrounded by a circle, often substitutes for coins in my readings as well, since it can represent material things. Seeing a plentiful number of these things might be a positive sign associated with a new job that has a higher income.

But sometimes it isn't that simple, and you know even before a reading that you won't be seeing a windfall of money coming your way. If you're facing foreclosure or debt, or if you're simply deciding how to invest money that you already have, you'll need to pay more attention to which symbols are associated with that money. If you see coins or pentacles, look around them in your crystal for clues about what is happening with the money. Is it changing hands? Do you recognize the people involved? Are there seasonal symbols that indicate a time frame, or a sign of investments being planted or harvested?

Numbers are of particular significance when you are reading on money matters. They can represent a sum of money or a date by which money may arrive or depart from your life. Don't be afraid to trust your first assumption when seeing the numbers, or to relate both potential meanings when reading for another person. For extra information, you may wish to review the numerological meanings of the numbers you see.

Relocation

When deciding whether you or somebody else should move to a certain area, the crystal ball can be a valuable tool. If you already have areas in mind, you can ask for a *yes* or *no* indication and look for symbols that are positive or negative to you. This can be highly individual. For example, while one person might see a spider as a household resident and a protector against flies, another person may find a spider threatening or sinister.

The true value of the crystal ball is that it can show you actual pictures of your future home. You would be surprised at how quickly you might forget the revelations though, especially if you have preconceived notions. So, record them quickly before they fade from memory. Create a quick sketch or, at the very least, note specific details that will help you identify one home or landmark from another.

If you are completely open to the area to which you might move, the crystal ball might tip you off to priorities in your life that you should keep in mind. For example, seeing money symbols might tip you off that financial considerations are key, or finding a job first might help you direct yourself to the correct location. Seeing images of your children might show you that school districts or future plans of your family could help guide your decision. Images of other people or family members who live a distance from you might be drawing you to consider living more closely.

Travel

Travel is often represented in the crystal ball even before the awareness of the person who is asking for advice. Take note if you see a symbol that tends to move from one place to another. If it is a car, or even a horse, it can represent travel over land. If it is a boat, then travel over a lake, river, or ocean may be indicated. If it is an airplane or even a bird, there may be travel through the air in a client's future. Images of distant friends or family members near such symbols may suggest taking a trip to visit these people.

Usually, when another person is asking me about a trip that has been planned already, it is simply for peace of mind about the safety of the trip. In these cases, seek symbols that may be either threatening or protective. In this situation, as in many others, animals may be shown. Think carefully about whether you find that animal either protective or threatening, and if you are reading for another, you may wish to ask him or her about such associations. For example, to one person a bear could be seen as a protective mother bear or as a teddy bear. But to someone else, a bear may seem very dangerous indeed.

Certainly some might ask if there is a specific symbol that portends danger on a trip. There is no one sign that tells you that you should cancel your reservations in the Bahamas. However, you should always trust your gut. If you see an image of your plane going down and your heart and soul tells you it isn't just a symbol, then go with that feeling. Even if nothing happens, your mind can rest at ease considering that something could have happened if you had not chosen your own destiny.

Self-esteem and self-worth issues

When reading for yourself, the crystal ball can act as a sort of therapist. You can share issues that you may not wish to reveal to anyone else. As such, it is especially important to record in a journal any reading that you do as a psychological exercise. Such symbols may repeat over time as you work through the issues at hand. People or animals represented may act as personal spirit guides or angels.

You might even see yourself undertaking actions that you have not yet done. This might be disturbing to see at first. If you see things that make you feel inspired, think of the crystal ball as a mirror that shows you what could happen. If what you see scares you or makes you feel disgusted, think of the crystal ball as a way to explore actions that you could have taken, but which might not seem like such a good idea anymore.

As you record your private readings in your journal, be careful to record not only the symbol and the meaning you interpreted at the time, but also your emotional reaction to the symbol and any tangential thoughts that may have occurred. Sometimes the process of this can be more fulfilling and cathartic than the outcome of the reading itself. For example, seeing a deceased family member in the crystal ball can bring feelings of both elation at laying eyes on this relative again as well as feelings of loss or disappointment about that which was left unsaid at your last meeting. Explore those feelings and talk them out with your crystal ball.

Trouble with children

If you're a parent like me, you may feel as though you need a little divine guidance. This may be especially true to get through the toddler and teen years. I've read for very small children indeed, but unless your kid has come to you with a specific concern, it may be best to focus on yourself and what you can do about the situation at hand instead of trying to pry deep into the mind of another person.

Pay extra special attention to how you ask your questions as it pertains to your own children. Even if you want to solve all of their problems, try to come at it from the point of view of what you can do to support your kids. Look for specific people who might be consulted, because often the crystal ball can alert you both to friends who can act as resources as well as to enemies who might do your children more harm than good.

If your kids come to you for a crystal ball reading, it can be a very special bonding experience. You can read with your child, rather than to your child, in order for it to not feel like yet another lecture. After all, your own feelings about the issue will no doubt tint the way you read. If you see your daughter's boyfriend, who doesn't meet your approval, you might describe him as looking sinister, and ignore the heart-shaped symbol of love he holds in his hand. Instead, try to state the facts as you see them, and perhaps ask your child what he or she thinks of each symbol as it comes through before offering your own feelings.

Health

Even though a crystal ball reading is neither a necessary nor sufficient replacement for the advice of a medical professional, you may find yourself using readings in a complementary way for yourself or a family member when journeying through a difficult health issue. I've seen symbols in the crystal ball that are helpful in a number of ways when used in health readings.

In the case of a difficult diagnosis process—during which many doctors have been consulted, test results are still coming in, and the root causes are still unknown—the crystal ball may indicate the afflicted body part or organ on a person shown within the crystal ball by showing a colored glow surrounding the culprit. (Such a colored glow, by the way, is a result of the *prism effect.* The crystal breaks white light into other colors and projects them at the eye. Some of the occlusions may seem like rainbows, while others may appear to be more prominently one color or another along the light spectrum.)

For example, a woman with kidney disease may be shown in the crystal ball with red or black smoke appearing around her lower abdomen, or the kidneys themselves may be shown as oddly colored objects inside of her.

The crystal ball can also offer a spiritual insight into physical illnesses for a more holistic approach to healing that takes into account your mind, body, and soul. For example, you may see in the crystal ball a family member, artistic pursuit, religious obligation, or lost love that could be affecting your health if you are neglecting that part of your life. Taking a look at your life from the perspective of the crystal ball can help you see what areas may be out of balance. You may be over-focused in one area such as work or service to a loved one, and that may be taking its toll on your health. Allow what you see in the crystal ball to be your wake-up call if one is desperately needed.

Confronting a bully

The most frustrating times in our lives are those in which crystal ball readings can be most helpful. If you feel completely helpless at the hands of a merciless bully in your life—such as an overbearing boss, an intolerable coworker, or even a demanding lover or teenaged child—the crystal ball can reveal helpful tips. In many readings that I will show you, the reader asks the crystal ball how to solve the situation. However, if you already envision how to deal with the bully, the crystal ball can also be used to explore several scenarios and allow them to play themselves out before your eyes.

For example, imagine a situation in which a woman is being sexually harassed by her boss at a job she otherwise loves. She is a strong person who doesn't take nonsense in her life, so her immediate temptation is to confront the boss angrily and possibly leave the job right then and there. After all, she can get a better job elsewhere. But she also knows that she could take the situation to Human Resources and see if they do right by her, so that she doesn't have disruption in an otherwise idyllic career path.

Such a woman could ask the crystal ball to play out each scene in front of her in order to see their potentials. If the crystal ball reveals an inept human resources department or an appealing new job, her decision may be swayed one way. If the crystal ball reveals a prompt and excellent response by Human Resources, her mind may be swayed in the other direction.

Examples from Real Readings

In the following section you'll read notes taken from real readings. Though they weren't transcribed directly word for word, since I took out all the dialogue that doesn't deal directly with symbol interpretation (which, by the way, makes the interpretations here appear to arrive much more rapidly and "on top of each other" than they really did!), you will be able to view what the symbols meant in each context and see how some signs can pop up again and again to reveal similar or different truths, depending on the people involved.

In these example readings, I often did know some details that people volunteered, so don't be discouraged that your readings don't always have such specifics if you are reading for those who are not so chatty. People usually come to me with questions that include details, or they unload a situation on me before we begin. I don't prevent them from speaking, but I do tell them that I need no further information in order to start their reading—though they are welcome to share whatever they fell compelled to share.

I tend to talk very fast during my readings and give lots of information without giving the person for whom I am reading much of a chance to reply. Your style may vary from mine, and that's okay. Remember, too, that I have done countless crystal ball readings, so if the flow of your reading is shorter than mine, longer than mine, or includes more process time as you talk out what you think might be going on, that's all right, too. That helps you become a better reader, or simply become the type of reader that you are meant to be.

Notice that it is okay to give more than one meaning to a symbol if it comes to you at the time. However, even if you know a symbol has two or more meanings, if only one of them seems clear to you, don't be afraid to stick with your first impulse. Remember that the crystal ball is a tool to aid your own intuition. Sometimes we second-guess ourselves right out of the correct answer. That's human nature, but my best advice to you in order to avoid that common trap is to simply conduct more readings.

The more you practice, the more you will gain confidence in your own skills and abilities, and the more well-versed you will be about your own symbols. Soon enough, if you choose to read for others, you'll find yourself standing your ground even when somebody objects to your interpretation. Your satisfaction will come later on when that person returns to you, admitting that you had been entirely correct and that it was their own judgment, rather than the crystal ball, that was clouded.

Again, the example readings here have been edited for brevity, so don't be intimidated by the speed at which the symbols come to you through this text. *You can and should take your time during your own readings!* Rest assured that even we experts have to slowly talk through our thoughts and pause to gather understanding during the flow of a real crystal ball reading. The examples that follow are just the "juicy bits" of the readings, with the other, slower bits of dialogue taken out.

Reading for a woman selling a home after a breakup

When I look into the crystal ball for you, the first symbol I see is a bird flying to the left. There may be some issues in the past that do need to be gently revisited. Perhaps there is somebody you need to get a hold of that you haven't talked to in a long time. There are also some past projects that you have abandoned, but taking them up again may help you make peace with yourself. I see a tulip, which promises a time of renewal and love for you during this upcoming spring, so make sure the ground is ready for that to grow. There is a gun pointing to the right that advises you to focus your energy more directly in the future. Be careful not to spread yourself so thin. Rather, prioritize what are the most important problems and then strike them down one by one. A sailboat indicates that there may be travel over water, or, more metaphorically, you may need to work on the journey of emotions that happens when you share with other people. Make sure that you are giving just as much as you are receiving.

Reading for a woman experiencing a bad family situation

The first symbol that I see is a broken heart, which can represent miscommunication that can lead to heartbreak. At times there can be a disconnect between the head and the heart, and one can begin to be too smart for their own good and especially for their own tongue! Be careful with your messages to others, especially when not in person, face to face.

I see a hand dropping a coin into a well. It seems as though one person may be doing more investment than another. This could mean investment of time, effort, or money, and it can be frustrating when there seems to be very little return. Try to make sure the sharing is a bit more equal, which may mean waiting before giving more or waiting before getting more!

I see a turkey facing to the right, which may represent a Thanksgiving in the future. This might mean some actions of significance need to take place this coming Thanksgiving, or, more metaphorically, it may mean that you have to reach out to someone in order to express your appreciation more thoroughly.

I see a bird sitting on a boat. It seems that somebody may be limited from their true fullest expression. There needs to be a way to find a meeting ground somewhere in between, a compromise. In some cases that might mean that you have to talk with somebody head to head rather than heart to heart! Both these symbols can also indicate travel.

I see a tree with branches reaching low to the ground. There are significant issues from the past that need to be worked through, and that might mean reaching back to your roots in more than one way. There may be an activity that you've enjoyed in the past that needs to be revisited again now.

I see the capital letter *P*, which may have significance to you. Sometimes this can be a letter in a person's name who is somebody you need to connect with. I also see a letter *C*, which may also have significance.

I see a triangle pointing up, which can represent three people or the gathering together of minds to collaborate on something. Take time out to celebrate, perhaps with friends, and bounce ideas off each other. One may give you good advice about how to rise above your situation, or help you network toward a common goal.

I see the number *1*. Numerologically, this may mean that you have to decide when to more aggressively pursue something and when to remain aloof. Choose your battles wisely!

Reading for a man wondering which creative endeavors to pursue

The first symbol I saw for you in the crystal ball was a hat. Usually this represents taking on a new role, sometimes a leadership role. In the course of developing your creative abilities, you may find yourself teaching others.

I see a horn of plenty, a cornucopia. That can represent abundance and creativity, making something out of nothing. It may also represent an instrument you may have played as a child that you might not play anymore.

A seashell reminds you that no matter which methods of art you use to display what is inside you, make sure that you are using your creativity to express your emotions and light up that same emotion inside others.

I see a hand gripping a pen. At some point in your life you may have found writing to be an inner talent of yours. This crystal suggests that you have it in you to write a book!

An alligator hiding halfway in and halfway out of the water shows that your drive to create will be lifelong, but urges you not to hide your work from others due to nervousness about your ability.

I see a snowflake turn into a flower. By the time winter turns to spring, you will have started on a new project. Don't abandon or question it at that time.

I see a shield. It may be a recurring battle in your life that you are good at starting things but maybe not so good at following through with them. It will be important for you to push past this.

I see an owl. Some of your best work will be done during odd hours. Also, you may find yourself undergoing your own self-directed study to increase your talents.

I see a mushroom. Along with the shield, this indicates that there may be some others who won't approve of or support you along the way, or might even wish to use your energies for their own means. Be careful about taking on the projects of others as your own.

Finally, there is the seed of a maple tree. You may begin with one mode of creativity, like writing, and the more you focus it, the more you lay seeds for other creative projects at other times and places in your life. What begins as one thing may turn into something totally different.

Reading for a divorcée supporting extended family

I see a dove flying to the left. This may indicate that you need to communicate with somebody in your past, possibly to make peace. Be sure that you've said all that you need to say currently to family members and that there is no unfinished business there weighing on your mind.

A tulip blooming indicates a new project that will begin for you this coming spring. Be ready for an emotional time!

I see the number *2*, which may be significant for you in the future. Keep your eye out and pay attention to any "second" choices that may be given to you.

I see a hat, which reiterates what your tarot reading said about taking on a leadership role. It may feel uncomfortable at first, but pay attention to the things that you do that cause other people to follow in your footsteps.

I see an apple, which is a symbol of the fruit of knowledge. You may undergo a course of study or put yourself through vigorous learning that will help your career.

I see a horse running to the right, which may indicate travel or a journey. The number *3* is by the horse, which may have significance as to when the travel is best to begin or end.

I see a comb, which means that you can often become caught up in the details instead of paying attention to what is truly important. Don't worry about what others think of you: just choose the most important thing and pursue your goals one at a time.

I see an elephant with its trunk raised toward the right, which is a good symbol for happy times ahead. It also encourages you to help your own memory. Take notes or start a journal if you haven't already.

Finally, I see a flag, which can represent nationality. Sometimes this comes when you might travel to another country. Or it might symbolize that it is important to go back to your roots at this time in your life.

Reading on a college student hoping to reconnect with a guy she was obsessed with last year

Your first symbol is an apple, which represents that this year knowledge and learning will be important to you, and is consistent with your desire to see him at school. There is a heart underneath the apple, but be careful: there is a crack in the heart! A cracked heart warns you to be careful with communications, so that they do not lead to heartbreak!

I see a tree with many branches growing upward. Be sure to be grateful to your roots and your family this year. You will actually have many love potentials coming, and your challenge will be to let yourself be open to the right ones!

I see a doorknob, which suggests that your plans for work or finances may change for the better in the long term. A door represents a new door opening in the material world.

I see a bell, which represents a call to action. Don't miss your chance when asked, even if you are not sure if the question is truly being asked. Make sure that you take the hint and at least follow up on it.

Keep your eyes out for a guy with dark, curly hair who either plays or has played the guitar. He will be a healing influence in your life and you might just find a spark there.

I see an arrow pointing up. This can sometimes indicate that you will travel. It also shows your ambitions and warns you not to be too hard on yourself. You can be a perfectionist!

I see a daffodil. This spring flower can represent a significant love potential that can grow during the next spring.

I see a boat. Make sure that you're making equal efforts to communicate. If only one person is putting in the effort, it can breed resentment, even in yourself! Let yourself share more by giving or taking less if necessary.

Reading on a man seeking help with his job working with troubled youth

The first thing I saw for you in my crystal ball was a hand holding an upside-down broken heart. I think there may be some miscommunication, possibly with a young male, which may not be able to be resolved in a usual way. Part of what you may need to do is model good behavior and support healing over time. I also see the letter *B* from his name next to a strawberry. This can represent summer, but it also represents a reward: fruits of a job well done that may be needed here. It can be hard for you to keep up your own efforts when you're not being rewarded appropriately. I see a gun pointing to the right being checked with a hand. Make sure you're using the right "ammunition" for the job. Some risks may need to be taken.

I see a rabbit looking to the right. You need to be able to express your creativity more in your work. This can mean injecting more creation and generation into current projects, or it can indeed mean moving to another workplace. I see a horn pointing to the left. It is time to listen to advice from somebody from your past. There may be some good networking available from this person, or just action that may be hard to take but is necessary. I see the capital letter *L*, so keep your eyes open for that in association with an opportunity. I see a sword, which can represent teaching or writing that springs from past conflicts. I think that part of your journey to where you are needs to be shared with others, and that could be the new beginning you're seeking. I see a sailboat, which can represent a physical journey to a new workplace, in addition to a journey of emotions.

Reading for a woman deciding whether the man she is with is "the one"

I see a young male deer walking to the right. Although, in many ways, the person you are with is wise, there's also an immature streak here to be aware of that is deeply seated. Sometimes, taking on the relationship as a playful challenge rather than an all-or-nothing endeavor, as you usually undertake things, may help.

I see a bell next to a feather. Do not ignore an inner call. No matter how loud you ring a bell at a feather, the sound will not push it away. Likewise, you must know whether you are using the right approach to your goals. I can see that, if this relationship does end, it will be you who ends it.

I see a broom, which does indicate the potential for marriage. Things can't always be easy, of course, with everything falling into your lap, but the potential for continuation long term exists if you choose for that to happen. It is up to you to decide whether this is worth the time and investment!

I see a wing. There are some efforts here that are one-sided, one giving much more than the other. This must be evened out to avoid resentment in the long run. This may mean waiting before giving more, or waiting before receiving more.

I see a heart next to an apple. There is love here, which is always good to see! There's also a learning experience here. And the fruits of this relationship can have an impact on other areas of life was well.

I see a goat looking to the left. There are some sticky points from the past that need to be worked out. Both of you can be very stubborn! But there are some unhealthy patterns that need to be worked out, no matter how unpleasant, for a better future!

I see a dog, which represents loyalty here. You can be loyal to a fault! Make sure that your friends play an important role in your life at all times, as they can temper the hard times.

I see a hat. No more waiting for your partner to make a move! It looks like you're going to be the one taking the leadership role in this relationship.

Reading for a wife deciding whether or not to stay with her husband

I see an oak leaf falling. Even the strongest of foundations in the heart often must see changes of the seasons. Certainly, your marriage cannot continue in this current state. By next fall you will have seen the necessary changes, for better or for worse!

I see a capital letter *C* and a hand dropping a coin. One of you may be much more generous with time and energy and even finances than the other. This sort of disparity can cause resentment over the long term. A bird flying to the left indicates that there may be some mutual friends or family from the past you'll need to get in contact with who may have some very good advice for you.

I see a mushroom. It can be easy for one person to live off of the energies of another. Especially when one person is such a helper personality that they take on the burdens of others easily. Find a way to create healthy boundaries now.

I see a candle burning. You have the energies to create what you need in order to survive physically and emotionally. It will take your dynamic efforts to make what you need to have happen occur. I see a scythe cutting a blossom. It is indeed time to cut off some things that no longer serve you the way that they should. I also see a thimble on a hand. Make sure that you don't excessively tear yourself away from everything that this life holds for you.

From the symbols in your crystal, it does appear that there needs to be a parting of ways. I'm sorry that this reading could not be more positive for you.

Reading for a woman wanting to know how a specific guy feels toward her

I see a man waiting in a chair, which is a good sign for stability but is also a sign that things may not move very fast. I see a shoe pointing to the left. There may be some issues in the past that he may have had trouble walking away from. I see a crown that shows interest in you and respect for you as a person. It also may suggest that he take the lead.

I see a spade, representing that he is intelligent and finds you an intellectual equal. I see an upside-down cup. There is no love here yet, but there is caring and a potential. I see an extended hand holding a coin next to a burning candle. He finds you down-to-earth and friendly, but there's also a spark here. All good signs. When you are excited about something, it is easy for him to get excited, too.

Reading for a woman wondering if a specific man can soon be her lover and husband

I see a house, which represents stability and is a good sign for the two of you to be fixtures in each other's lives. However, I'm also seeing several travel symbols as well: a flag, which sometimes indicates international travel, and a bird flying to the right, indicating communication over a physical distance in the future.

I see a moon representing repeating cycles that may have happened for one or both of you in the past, which cause fear and may prevent the two of you from being together soon. It represents the need to end a cycle.

I see a lion waiting at a wall. It seems that there are some barriers to the two of you being together, and marriage has not yet been indicated. You are strong enough to wait in a relationship with these barriers, but it may not be good for you to do so since your strengths might be better recognized in another relationship.

I see two people back to back. There are other people and things distracting both of you right now from being together. Those issues must be resolved before you can face each other.

I see a gloved hand, representing that it may be tempting for one of you to keep an emotional distance in order to feel safe. There is also a dress, which may represent that you will need to take on a different role in his life.

I see an arrow pointing up and a cup, representing a lot of healing that needs to take place in order to reach a place of better understanding.

Reading for a woman wanting to know about anyone new coming into her life for love

I see a sun and many small seedlings sprouting. You will actually have several potentials that can come into your life and you can afford to be choosy when deciding on a love relationship. You have more than one "the one," fortunately! Be careful not to be too all-or-nothing in your dating. Instead, allow fun and friendship to grow, rather than being burnt out by being too intense. Nothing is going to be perfect, fall-in-your-lap easy, of course! The best love advantages are the ones physically local.

I see a man holding a book and wearing a suit. He has light-colored hair. The suit may represent that he has held a position of power or had to wear a uniform at some point in his life. The book may represent a strong intelligence and a love of working with ideas. I see another man playing a guitar. He has a slender build, and the guitar may represent creativity or that he has played guitar in the past.

I see a mushroom. Be careful that you do not get sucked into a relationship with a needy person. You can tend to be such a helper personality that you easily take on the burdens of others. I see a capital letter *E* that may be in a name. I see an explorer's hat representing someone who loves to travel and perhaps potential for you to travel with someone romantically in the near future.

Reading for a college student looking forward to having a career and a love life!

I see a man with dark hair wearing a hat, seated and holding an axe. These symbols may indicate an internship or other short-lived career opportunity that is a good idea for you to pursue. Look for short-term things that will help you build your experience while allowing you to escape them if they don't turn out to be something you want for the long run! Good networking can result!

I see a rocket taking off from an upside-down table. This can show that you need to find freedom before you can find stability. Get yourself clear from any obligations you no longer need, and that will allow your ambitions to take flight!

I see a hand offering a cup. Both love and happy job opportunities can start for you from friendships. Now is the time to extend a hand of friendship and make reasons to network and celebrate.

I see a horn above a graduation cap. Be quick to jump on opportunities offered right at graduation. Make sure you get yourself out there. Some of these opportunities may be gone quickly.

I see a bird sitting on a holly leaf and looking to the left. Next winter, make sure to communicate with people from your past who might have opportunities for you in the future.

Reading for a woman who just escaped a negative relationship in which she was not treated well

I see a woman in a cloak heading up a mountain with a lamp. It is important first to make room in your life for your next loving relationship, which may mean a time of feeling isolated or alone as a "hermit" to be happy with yourself and make sure that you will not choose somebody who can take advantage of you. Remember that you will have many options, so be careful not to choose the first man who comes along, as he may not be best.

I see a heart next to a water lily. Keep your eyes out this summer for a love opportunity.

I see a man with light-colored hair wearing a suit and hat. You may meet him in context with his work, not necessarily yours. Keep your eyes out for somebody who is a leader. He has his head bowed, showing that this is a man who will respect you greatly.

I see this man holding out a coin in his hand. Watch for early signs of generosity, as this person is one who is willing to give more effort than you may have been used to.

Reading for a woman wondering if her six-month relationship can progress

I see a shepherd's crook. You have done a good job of giving gentle guidance to him, but he still pulls away the more he feels like he is being drawn away from his old life, his old circle of friends, or the independence he values.

I see a ship's bell ringing. The kind of communication you are seeing now may feel unequal. You may be putting in much more effort than him. Unfortunately, I don't see much of a change on that front. The change you've seen is what you'll get, so decide carefully if it is enough. As the ship sails to the right, it is almost as if your decision has been made for you.

I see an arrow pointing to the right with a feather. Travel may be needed in the future for one or both of you to clear the head and get priorities straight.

I see an overturned cup. A feeling of loss and disappointment. It seems like there may be some resentment brewing, so make sure that you make choices and communicate clearly to avoid more hurt. Healing needs to begin.

I see a perched hawk. You've viewed things clearly, and you have waited for movement to happen. He has so much fear, though, that he has a hard time seeing things clearly. Even if it would be best for him to commit, he does not wish to.

I see a fish swimming toward the right. Trust your gut and act on your wisdom. Only you can change things in your life.

I see a heart next to a bare tree. He does care for you, and that isn't the problem. He just doesn't have the kinds of things to give to you that you truly want at this time. It isn't that he is holding out on you. He just feels incapable.

I see a hand holding an anchor. It seems that, if this relationship is to end, it will be you who ends it. But it has the potential to stay right where it is, if that is what you desire. Unfortunately, not much more progress is indicated at this time.

Reading for a man who has a strange presence, sensed by another psychic, with him

I see a broom next to a tree. The tree often indicates ancestral relations when shown in readings involving a deceased family member. The broom also represents a marriage relationship being very important. I see a capital letter *I* and a capital letter *G*, which may be in names or place names associated with the person.

I see a cup with a flame in it near a bell. You've had a call to creation within you. Sometimes the creativity shown can represent a child, but it can also be a more metaphorical creative call, usually one that involves healing. These symbols ask you not to ignore your inner calling, and to pursue them to manifest.

I see an open hand reaching up to a white rose. This indicates a need for generosity, and perhaps to reach out to an old friend from the past who may need emotional help or to reconnect.

I also see an arrow with two interlocking rings pointing to the right. It may be important to plan a trip to bring together two things that you have enjoyed either from your life's past or your ancestral past and your present.

Reading for a woman wanting to know what she should do during an internship to get hired

The first symbol I see is a salmon leaping to the right. The salmon is the symbol of knowledge and wisdom, so this internship will be a great learning experience indeed! Don't be afraid to try out things that you don't know quite how to do. The internship may actually lead to job opportunities that you can grow into, even if you are not prepared.

I see a boot balancing on a rock. Be careful about how many responsibilities you take on. You have a lot of passion and you're good at what you set your mind to; however, taking care of your own health will be key. As will spotting the opportunities that are stable and long term.

I see a flag, which has several meanings. Sometimes it can mean working with other countries or nationalities, even traveling there. The other meaning is to get back to your own ancestral roots during this process.

I see a capital letter *D*, which may be in a name of a person you should network with in order to land a good job.

I see a woman with long, blond hair who may also be a key player that you should get to know. She is holding a broom, which may represent that she is married but it can also represent somebody who has the power to clean out people and bring in people. She is wearing a uniform with a hat that represents leadership and a cross, which can represent a faith connection that she has, or it can also represent that she can offer you protection.

Reading for a woman who is nervous about searching for love

I see a many-branched tree growing out of a boot. You actually have several options for love ahead of you, so you needn't be worried so much about whether a person can be a love. Concentrate more on making careful choices about how far you want to take relationships with those you encounter! There may be some friends or even family of yours who know your patterns even better than you do who can help you with your choices!

I see a hat with wings. You'll need to take on a leadership role in pursuing some relationships. Have fun and enjoy the experience, which might mean dialing down the intensity so that you can have a thicker skin!

I see a man with dark hair and a horn. Even though trusting your gut keeps you busy with love interests, don't ignore those calls to action. A good relationship may be coming with somebody who once played, or still plays, a musical instrument. Sometimes this symbol can also represent meeting somebody in a creative and casual context. I see the capital letter *L*, which can represent a name. I see a palm tree, which can represent love of travel and a laid-back personality. I see a house, which represents valuing stability. If any of these descriptions fit your current crush, it may be a clue. However, several of these seem to be speaking toward another option, so don't get fixated on him as your only option.

I see a rabbit emerging from a hiding place. This can mean passionate love. It can also mean fertility, so if that's not in your plans for right now, be cautious!

Reading for a man wanting characteristics of women he should seek for love

I see the capital letter *N*. That may be a first or last initial or a place name.

I see a gun pointing to the left, indicating that you may need to rid yourself of past emotional baggage to be ready for a new relationship.

I see a woman with long, dark hair playing a flute. She may have played the flute in the past. Or the flute can also represent creativity. She is wearing a dress, which can represent that she has been married in the past or it can also mean that she has to hold a formal role at work.

I see a heart being planted with a spade. It may be important to establish yourself in the local community, even more than you have already, in order to be out there to pursue interesting women. The spade represents grounding activities—such as exercise, working with your hands, and being outdoors—as feeding your soul during this time.

I see a baby carriage near an apple, which may represent a woman who has children and teaches as part of her career role. I see a capital letter *E*, which again could be an initial or a place name.

Reading on a man who experienced abuse from an unknown assailant as a child

I immediately see a boat, showing that this man has communication issues. I also see an eagle symbol that looks very much like the eagle from the U.S. Postal Service logo. It could have something to do with his work or with how he interacted with others. I see the letter *C* in his name. Also a letter *I* is shown. I see a collared but short-sleeved shirt lying on a floor. He has trouble fitting into roles in his life and so he may have shifted through many of them. The number *3* is also shown to me. I see a mushroom, indicating that he uses many people throughout life at this time.

Reading on a woman's sister and her college, career, and love life

I see a cracked heart next to a bell and a rolling pin. It seems like there has been love in the relationship that your sister has. But that she's put far more effort in than the other person, and I'm afraid her love just doesn't seem to match his. He understands her feelings, loud and clear, but it seems as though he isn't answering the call to potential marriage. That bell has already sounded. I think she could do better by leaving that relationship than by waiting.

I see a bridge on fire! Though it may be slow going to finish college and start a career, things will pick up quickly once she has the right start! I see a couple number 1s, which may indicate 2011, eleven months, or that other things with the number 11 are going to be significant for changes in this realm.

I see a signpost next to a tree. There may be times when your sisters and you live temporarily in the same state, but the physical closeness may be transient.

I see a coin being thrown into a cup. Though your sister doesn't have a whole heap of money shown in her future career, there will be enough to get by, enough to share, and emotional riches beyond that!

Reading on a woman seeking love and choosing between three jobs

I see a high-heeled shoe, so I can tell that you will look like a professional fit for the jobs you're looking at. Of course it is up to you to choose the right one for you! I see a dancing person holding a flower, so I think that whatever job you choose, you will be drawn to dance as a creative outlet and a way to use your energy positively. Please continue to pursue Zumba! I also see you holding a book, indicating that you may have more learning or studying to do in that area. I see an apple, which is a sign for a doctor, so I think the job at the pediatrician's office is better than the telemarketing one, because it may offer more opportunities or be more long term—even if it is less money. You can do that until you find the right opportunity for Zumba!

I see a man with broad shoulders, and he may have light-colored hair but he is wearing a graduation cap, so I assume he will be associated with your school. He may be an important love relationship! I see a crab next to him, so his sign may be Cancer!

I see a sword with a flag on it, indicating that you are smart enough to do well in college for the fall semester. Keep your eyes out for a chance for travel that may come from your college interests, as it will be good for you!

Reading for a woman hoping to be in a relationship soon and wanting a gentleman described

I see a race car heading left. This may represent a gentleman who used to be quite daring—in fact, he may even have raced cars in his youth. But now he has matured a bit and is ready to slow down but still has a sense of adventure.

I see a light-haired man who is dressed like royalty. He is one who likes to take the lead. But this may be a different gentleman from the first since the symbols were a little distanced from each other.

I see a gun, which can represent decisive action and can also represent one who hunts—not only as a hobby but also someone who is searching for a woman! Be cautious of this one, though, as he may have a bad-boy streak.

Reading on a pregnant woman wanting to know about her pregnancy and her baby

I see a heart with a keyhole in it. You have many blessings in your life and people who love you. Yet the adventure is not complete. You may be searching for the perfect fit of things and people in your life, and along the way do not be disappointed when nothing completely stops the hunger for more. It is the journey rather than the destination!

I see a carrot in the earth. Take time for grounding activities for yourself. That can include working with your hands, exercising, and spending time in nature. These activities will feed your soul.

I see a child next to two musical instruments: a violin and a flute. This may be encouraging you to look into musical gifts early in the life of your baby. Listen to your favorite music frequently during this time!

I see a boat next to a tree. Keep up communication with any distant family members, even if it may seem one-sided at times. A connection to your roots is needed for you. Sometimes this can mean close family only, but it can also ask you to find ways to connect with things from your childhood or even your ancestors.

I see a sword. Overthinking things at this point is natural for you, but not always beneficial! Keep a journal, if you don't already, as intellectual pursuits will help occupy your busy mind with the best things!

Reading on a boyfriend that a woman suspects is not being totally honest with her

The first symbol I saw was a small airplane heading down. Your boyfriend tries to escape conflict with you by not being entirely truthful with you. That doesn't mean you shouldn't confront him, as this escapism is not a healthy power play on his part. But it does mean that you should be mindful of how you react and how you communicate with him about that which you may not be happy about.

I see a mountain climber with a pick. Your boyfriend has been trying to improve himself. But he feels that there is something lacking in your current relationship. It is important that you do talk with him about this and don't just leave things as they are—otherwise he might begin to take more drastic measures in order to try to figure out what's missing.

I see a bell. I think many of these actions he does may be for attention or almost a cry for help. A call to action. I see an arrow pointing toward a chair. He may be feeling unstable. Some of this may be related to work, or financial or physical matters. Though each of you seek some semblance of stability, your relationship takes on this confusing and unstable quality. I see a rose and a cup. There is caring here, so there is a potential for a loving future with him if you choose it. However, of course things won't be easy or perfect, so it will be important for you to continuously reevaluate whether he is worth your time and effort. I see a flame and a trowel. He may be engaging in some flirtation, but no serious love affair is indicated! It is important, though, for you to talk with him about your concerns, as otherwise the seeds may be planted for resentment.

Reading for a woman deciding whether and how to proceed with a relationship potential

The first symbol I see is a horseshoe, representing luck, but it is positioned in such a way as to encourage you to grab a chance while you can. This doesn't necessarily tell you to rush things, but it does ask you to keep vigilant for little ways to learn from him and his presence in your life.

I see a heart next to a leaf. This fall is an important time for your heart, and it is important to explore ways to push past old baggage and renew and heal yourself. This may be one reason you keep seeing him in your life. The heart is a good sign, as it represents that he has some interest and some feelings as well! I see a triangle with a flag at the top. He alone isn't the answer. Remember that this is about the journey, not the destination, and he is a waypoint along the way that it is important for you to see.

I see a face looking at a sword. You appreciate those on the same mental wavelength, and simple communication, even at a distance, over e-mail or on the phone, is a good place to start. Just make sure it is an aid to getting to know him rather than a barrier!

I see a broom, a bottle, and some torn clothing. There is a potential for long-term love here. However, past destruction in one or both of your lives may cause there to be some delay or hindrance to being able to give love fully at this time. It is definitely worth exploring, however.

Have Fun Reading the Crystal Ball

By now you've seen how crystal ball readings flow once you've learned how to perform them, and you've been given the tools to be able to start crystal ball reading right away. Don't be intimidated by the challenge, or worry that your crystal ball reading technique doesn't quite match up with mine. We are all unique people, and we see and understand things in different ways.

Once you get your own crystal ball, ground yourself, and open yourself up to the reading experience, you will be surprised and delighted at the many applications that this ancient art has to modern life. If you choose to bless the world by reading the crystal ball for others, you will be the newest ambassador for this rare but growing practice. That may make you feel responsible for providing quality readings, which is a good thing and can help you become a better reader. But remember also that this should all be fun!

The more you practice, the easier and more fun crystal ball reading will be for you. Good luck as you make discoveries about yourself, solve problems, and add to the living history of the practice of crystal ball reading.

glossary

Astral travel: Out-of-body experiences in which the source of one's perception seems to be on an imaginary or supernatural spiritual plane of existence that is separate from the earthly, physical realm.

Augur: One who performs crystal ball reading, or any other form of divination, by interpreting omens.

Augury: Divination, including use of the crystal ball.

Aura: A perceived color or several colors that surround a person, either in the crystal ball or in everyday life.

Binary response: Using divination to achieve a simple *yes* or *no* answer.

Centering: Gathering one's thoughts and being present in the moment. Usually performed after grounding.

Chakras: A system of visualizing chi centers within the body.

Channel: A person acting as a direct conduit for information coming from another source, such as the divine or a deceased person through possession. If one were channeling using a crystal ball, it would be the entity coming through who was using the tool, not the person acting as the vessel for the entity.

Character divination: Using a divination tool such as the crystal ball to confirm or discover character traits in the person being read, as opposed to simply studying the past, present, and future.

Chi: The medium through which life and change is manifested in the universe.

Clairaudience: Receiving messages through the perception of hearing.

Claircognizance: Having wise thoughts that do not seem to be your own and having clear-thought.

Clairsentience: Receiving perceptions through your emotions.

Clairvoyance: Seeing visions and having clear-sight.

Cold reading: The art of appearing to perceive more information about a person than you do.

Countercheck: Using a second crystal ball, a second reader, or any other type of divination to double-check the answers received during the primary consultation.

Crystal ball: A sphere made of pure crystal, usually quartz.

Crystalomancy: Fortunetelling using a crystal ball.

Divination: Using tools that are believed to discover the past, present, and future.

Divinatory response: Answers received during the practice of divination.

Diviner: One who practices divination.

Energy: For the purposes of this book, energy is the same as chi, not to be confused with the thermodynamic quantity used in physical science.

Ethereal travel: Out-of-body-experiences in which you are still perceiving the real world, but your senses of perception seem to be coming from a source outside of your body.

Forecast: A prediction of events or opportunities that may happen in the future.

Fortunetelling: Examining the past, present, future, and character of a person, with or without tools such as the crystal ball.

Gazing: Using a crystal ball or other scrying tool to divine the future, whether or not images are actually seen in the surface being examined.

Grounding: The process of pushing excess chi into the earth, and drawing needed chi from the earth, in order to prepare oneself or recover oneself from meditation or divination.

Hero's Journey: A story that follows a series of archetypes that is seen repeated within the analysis of many stories across cultures and times.

Hypothesis: An idea you have about the way something is or how something works that you can then test to find evidence of whether it is true or not.

Numerology: Divination using numbers. This can be practiced on numbers seen within the crystal ball.

Omen: A sign seen, usually accidentally, that is believed to have meaning. For example, an unusual flash of light seen in the crystal ball because of the setting of the sun.

Oracle: A historical term for a person or mythological figure who produces prophecies directly from divine sources through possession or channeling.

Ornithomancy: Divination using the activities of birds. Since birds are often seen in the crystal ball, ornithomancy has practical applications to their placement and behavior within it.

Palmistry: Palmistry is the practice of reading the lines and lumps of the hands. Your hands are almost like your own personal GPS for life, since characteristics of your hands change over time.

Pendulum dowsing: The pendulum is a *plumb-bob*, an object hung on a string. When dangled from one hand, it swings freely. A pendulum can be used on a location to indicate a direction, and many pendulum charts or maps can be used to all sorts of purposes, much in the same way as a Ouija board is a chart on which the planchette can indicate letters, numbers, and a negative and affirmative answer.

Presage: An answer from divination that is perceived as referencing the future.

Prognostication: A declaration of an answer received through divination.

Prophecy: A divine message.

Prophet: One who delivers a prophecy.

Psychic: A person who perceives things by means other than the usual five senses.

Psychic vampire: A person who upsets the balance of your chi, usually by draining it. The efforts of psychic vampires, whether accidental or on purpose, can be countered by grounding and shielding.

Reading: A term for the act of divination.

Response: An answer, either literal or figurative, from divination, such as with the crystal ball.

Scryer: One who practices scrying.

Scrying: The practice by which literal or symbolic images are seen that are believed to have meaning and purpose.

Séance: The practice by which the dead are contacted for communication.

Seer: A fortuneteller. The term usually implies visual methods such as crystal ball reading, dream interpretation, or clairvoyance.

Shewstone: Sometimes synonymous with a crystal ball, a shewstone does not have to be spherical or made of crystal.

Shielding: The practice of protecting one's chi from contamination by the chi of another person, place, or event.

Sitting: A divination session.

Soothsayer: Meaning *truth sayer*, this is a somewhat archaic word for one who practices divination.

Subconscious mind: A term that describes the consciousness experienced when asleep and dreaming, or in a deep meditative state, as well as the unconscious understandings at work during normal waking life.

Symbolic response: An answer received during divination that is figurative rather than literal.

Symbolic thought: Interpretation of symbols perceived during divination.

Tarot: The tarot is a deck of seventy-eight cards that can each represent archetypes of characters found along the classic Hero's Journey, elements that are found in nearly every good story. When they are laid out in specific patterns called *spreads*, the cards can reflect your own story in divination or meditation.

Third-party readings: When you read for somebody who is not present—for example, if a friend comes to you and asks you how her boyfriend feels about her. An ethical issue here is that the boyfriend is not giving his permission to be read.

Visualization: Mentally envisioning pictures with your mind's eye.

bibliography

Andrews, Ted. *Crystal Balls & Crystal Bowls*. Woodbury, MN: Llewellyn Publications, 2008.

Campbell, Joseph. *Myths to Live By*. New York: Penguin Putnam, 1972.

————. *The Hero with a Thousand Faces*. New York: Bollingen Foundation, 1949.

Castaneda, Carlos. T*he Teaching of Don Juan: A Yaqui Way of Knowledge*. New York: Washington Square Press, 1968.

Cunningham, Scott. *Divination for Beginners*. St. Paul, MN: Llewellyn Publications, 2003.

Huxley, Aldous. *The Doors of Perception.* New York: Harper & Row, 1954.

Jung, Carl. *Man and His Symbols.* Garden City, NY: Doubleday & Company, 1964.

McElroy, Mark. *Lucid Dreaming for Beginners.* Woodbury, MN: Llewellyn Publications, 2007.

Mirabello, Mark. *A Séance Procedure.* Portsmouth, OH: Other World Society, 2009.

Silbey, Uma. *Crystal Ball Gazing: The Complete Guide to Choosing and Reading Your Crystal Ball.* New York: Fireside, 1998.

TED ANDREWS

CRYSTAL BALLS & CRYSTAL BOWLS

TOOLS FOR ANCIENT SCRYING
&
MODERN SEERSHIP

Crystal Balls & Crystal Bowls

Tools for Ancient Scrying & Modern Seership

TED ANDREWS

Quartz crystal balls and crystal bowls are popular magical tools. Yet not everyone understands the extent of their power and multipurpose potential. Ted Andrews reveals how these dynamic instruments can be used for divination, astral projection, spirit communication, healing, and reaching higher states of consciousness.

You will learn many methods of crystal gazing, along with ways to enhance this practice with candles, fragrances, and elixirs. Also included are techniques for divining with water, communicating with angels and spirit guides, developing clairvoyance, and activating creativity. This updated edition also contains new illustrations.

978-1-56718-026-8, 256 pp., 6 x 9   **$15.95**

To order, call 1-877-NEW-WRLD
Prices subject to change without notice
Order at Llewellyn.com 24 hours a day, 7 days a week!

Divination

For Beginners

Reading the Past, Present & Future

SCOTT CUNNINGHAM

Divination for Beginners

Reading the Past, Present & Future

SCOTT CUNNINGHAM

There's no need to visit a soothsayer or call a psychic hotline to glimpse into your future or to uncover your past. You can become your own diviner of things unseen with the many methods outlined in this book, written by popular author Scott Cunningham.

Here you will find detailed descriptions of both common and unusual divinatory techniques, each grouped by the tools or techniques used to perform them. Many utilize natural forces such as water, clouds, smoke, and the movement of birds. Also discussed are the more advanced techniques of Tarot, palmistry, and the I Ching.

978-0-7387-0384-8, 264 pp., 5 $^3/_{16}$ x 8 $13.95

To order, call 1-877-NEW-WRLD
Prices subject to change without notice
Order at Llewellyn.com 24 hours a day, 7 days a week!